GROUND COVERS
For Easier Gardening

Bird's Foot
Violet

GROUND COVERS

FOR EASIER GARDENING

By DANIEL J. FOLEY

Photographs by
PAUL E. GENEREUX
AND OTHERS

Line Drawings by
CHARLOTTE EDMANDS BOWDEN

Hepatica

CHILTON COMPANY · BOOK DIVISION

Publishers

PHILADELPHIA AND NEW YORK

Designed by William E. Lickfield

Manufactured in the United States of America

To

Charlotte Edmands Bowden
and

Paul E. Genereux

Contents

Acknowledgments

Those who have shared with me four decades of gardening "ups and downs" have in large measure prompted the making of this book.

To DOROTHY S. GARFIELD, for typing the manuscript, preparing the index, and handling countless details with skill, patience, and devotion, I am greatly indebted.

To CHARLOTTE EDMANDS BOWDEN for the drawings which enhance this book, and to PAUL E. GENEREUX for the majority of the photographs, collected over a period of years, are due a large measure of gratitude. They have shared their knowledge, skill, and enthusiasm with the writer for a total of twenty-five years, and it is fitting that this book should be dedicated to them.

To Dr. G. L. LAVERTY, who first permitted me to experiment with ground covers in his garden a quarter of a century ago, I am most grateful for the encouragement and the stimulus he offered. Likewise, to Mr. and Mrs. JOHN STAPF, JR., who shared their garden with me in the pursuit of my study of low-growing plants.

To Miss HELEN A. H. BERRY, who made the color illustrations, and to Mr. ARNO H. NEHRLING, Director of Publications, Massachusetts Horticultural Society, for permission to reproduce them, I am most grateful.

To Mrs. ARTHUR ADAMS; Mrs. OLIVER AMES; ARNOLD ARBORETUM; RALPH BAILEY; WOODBURY BARTLETT; Mrs. JOSEPH BATCHELDER; Mrs. E. A. BOLLONG; Mr. and Mrs. HAROLD C. BOOTH; *The Boston Globe;* Mr. and Mrs. ALBERT L. BROWN; STEDMAN BUTTRICK; ANDREW BYE; Mrs. FREDERICK CARDER; Mrs. STEPHEN R. CASEY; Mr. and Mrs. JOHN CASKEY; CLARENDON GARDENS; COLONIAL WILLIAMSBURG, INC.; CHARLES H. P. COPELAND; CORLISS BROTHERS, INC.; Dr. and Mrs. MARCUS E. COX; RODERICK W. CUMMING; JAN DE GRAAFF; HOMER DODGE; KENNETH DRAYER; Dr. and Mrs. ROBLEY D. EVANS; Mrs. W. W. K. FREEMAN; Miss

9

ELEANOR GARDNER; THE GARDNER MUSEUM; LEONARD H. GARFIELD; Mr. and Mrs. JOHN W. GORDON; Mr. and Mrs. C. A. B. HALVORSON, JR.; Mrs. LAURA HATTON; BETTY JANE HAYWARD; KARL HOBLITZELLE; JACKSON & PERKINS CO.; KELSEY-HIGHLANDS NURSERY; Mr. and Mrs. JAMES LAWRENCE, JR.; MILFORD LAWRENCE; Mr. and Mrs. OTTO LIPMAN; Mrs. PHILIP LORD; Mr. and Mrs. HOLLIS LOVELL; Miss C. SALLY LOW; Miss KATHERINE V. LYFORD; J. HORACE MCFARLAND COMPANY; Mrs. BRUCE J. MCLAUGHLIN; DOROTHY S. MANKS and the STAFF of the MASSACHUSETTS HORTICULTURAL SOCIETY LIBRARY; MASSACHUSETTS HORTICULTURAL SOCIETY; H. GLEASON MATTOON; Mrs. MCINTOSH MERRILL; Mr. and Mrs. GEORGE S. MOORE; ARNO H. NEHRLING; DANIEL J. O'BRIEN; Mrs. GEORGE S. PARKER; Mr. and Mrs. STEPHEN PHILLIPS; ROBINSON GARDENS; FRANCES DIANE ROBOTTI; Mr. and Mrs. JOHN P. ROCHE; HAROLD S. ROSS; the STAFF of the SALEM PUBLIC LIBRARY; Dr. and Mrs. CHARLES P. SHELDON; Mr. and Mrs. GILBERT L. STEWART, JR.; GEORGE TALOUMIS; Mrs. GEORGE E. TAYLOR; Mr. and Mrs. LUCIEN B. TAYLOR; THOMSON NURSERY; Mr. and Mrs. ABBOTT PAYSON USHER; MARINUS VAN DER POL; ARTHUR S. WARD; WAYSIDE GARDENS; Mr. and Mrs. MAURICE WEINER; Mrs. FRANCES WILLIAMS; and Mr. and Mrs. JOHN WORDEN, who have contributed in various ways by sharing their gardens for photographing, their professional skills and their efforts, I am most appreciative.

To my family and to countless garden enthusiasts whose forbearance and patience I have constantly tested in preparing the material for this book I am indebted beyond measure.

DANIEL J. FOLEY

Salem, Massachusetts

Introduction

The beginnings of this book go back nearly forty years to the time when, as a small boy, I planted a garden on a hillside. It had been a part of a rough pasture and was separated from the surrounding area by a low stone wall. Witch grass had made inroads for a number of years, and it took a heap of digging to remove it. But, not all the witch grass was eliminated on the first try.

Creeping phlox, hardy alyssum, arabis, a few cotoneasters, and some spreading junipers were planted to hold the soil on this rather steep slope. The perennials bloomed and flourished, the cotoneasters and the junipers took hold, and so, too, did the remaining roots of the witch grass. This experience comes to mind every time the use of ground covers is mentioned, for it is a common experience when planting rough ground. Weeds and all their roots must be eliminated before a good start can be made with ground covers. Thorough preparation at the start is one of the steps toward easier gardening with any kind of plant.

The year-round beauty of heather and its adaptability to hot, dry, rocky soil first came to my attention when I saw a clump growing in an open pasture in East Boxford, Massachusetts. The trail of the heather then took me to a garden in the sand dunes of nearby Ipswich. In later years, visits to picturesque gardens on Cape Cod, where the soil is light and sandy, provided opportunity for further study of ground covers. There, on the side of a slope, heather was planted in broad drifts, and what a joy it was on that hot August day. There had been no rain for weeks, and yet the heather bloomed in all its glory and the bees hovered round. The heather was content and at home. Several years later, I spent many pleasant days inspecting all kinds of heather in gardens in Seattle, Washington, and Portland, Oregon.

Trips to Williamsburg, Virginia, Pinehurst, North Carolina, to the country gardens of Maine and Vermont, the Jersey sand dunes and the Pennsylvania woodlands, revealed an infinite variety of plant material for carpeting the soil in gardens.

In the woodlands of Killarney, Ireland, where the rhododendrons of the Himalayas and tropical plants from South America grow in wild abandon, carpeted beneath with drifts of heather and gorse skirting the edges of every planting and bordering the roadsides, there is proof of Nature's embellishment of man's efforts to create a natural effect with ground covers.

A keener appreciation of perennials resulted from frequent conversations with Mrs. Frances Williams, noted horticulturist, who began collecting plantain-lilies, or hostas, many years ago and assembling them in her small garden in Winchester, Massachusetts. As her hobby grew, she also gathered many native plants and cultivated kinds with variegated foliage that would grow in the shade. As is often the case with gardeners, Mrs. Williams shared her plants and her experiences with the author.

Seven years of gardening at Breeze Hill, in Harrisburg, Pennsylvania, with that eminent horticulturist and great plantsman, the late J. Horace McFarland, opened up new horizons for the use of ground covers. The Memorial Rose and Max Graf were planted on shady banks. One of the most rewarding ground cover combinations of all was Hills-of-snow hydrangea and the Canadian violet, intermingled with plantain-lilies and clumps of leucothoe. This combination grew on a broad bank under spruce trees.

In shady parts of Breeze Hill Gardens there were quantities of ferns interplanted with clumps of wood hyacinths which blossomed profusely in late spring. In summer, under many of the shrub roses, the Hanson lily came up through ground covers. These included foam-flower, pachysandra, myrtle, ivy, sweet woodruff or some other low-growing plant, but always these lilies persisted and showed off to great advantage above their green carpet.

Several trips to the Northwest opened up the treasures in the great gardens of Oregon and Washington. A similar experience resulted from a trip to California. In Seattle it was my pleasure to visit Lilla Leach, who introduced *Kalmiopsis leachiana*. Her garden was truly a wild one, a bower of beauty, dripping with all the choice native plants of the Northwest, massed in broad drifts. Other notable gardens opened the way to broader horizons for the use of ground covers. It was in Oregon and in British Columbia that I first saw the golden-tasseled St. Johnswort carpeting banks in the shade of trees. Several trips through Canada, from Quebec to Ottawa and Hamilton, visiting home gardens, public parks and botanic gardens, some famous for their alpine plants, showed what could be accomplished with ground covers.

Thirty years of lecturing to enthusiastic members of garden clubs have made me even more aware of the fact that a simple book on ground-cover plants, replete with pictures emphasizing their use, was needed to make gardening easier and more pleasurable. Here it is.

DANIEL J. FOLEY

Salem, Massachusetts

I

Ground Covers—What Are They?

Ground covers are Nature's carpets that clothe soil in a variety of green array and make this flowering world all the brighter and more beautiful. As Ernest H. Wilson, noted plant hunter and benefactor of gardens, has expressed it, "Mother Nature—economical yet paradoxically extravagant—provides in abundance plant material for clothing all but the most arid and frigid regions of the globe. The depths of the tropical forests are carpeted with a wondrous miscellany of plants, the open treeless areas of the world with grasses and herbs in great variety, the alpine regions with herbs and low shrubs, endless in species, which usually bear richly colored flowers, the boreal regions of the world with low, trailing, stem-rooting plants, many of which are evergreen in character. For us who garden in northern lands, these boreal plants of compact habit and low stature have a value beyond price."

Aside from their beauty, these carpeting plants check the forces of erosion and prevent the sun and the wind from making our world a barren planet. Through eons of time many of them have adapted themselves to the exposed and unprotected parts of the earth's surface, often surviving in meager soil of the poorest quality. Some of the tiniest gems that thrive in the crevices of our terraces and walks have come to us from the moist, mountain meadows on the very roof of the world. Others that we use as cover plants are native in fields and pastures and along the wayside. And there are those that flourish on the edges of streams or are splashed by the salt spray as they bind the shifting sands. We grow them in our gardens to serve the same purpose that they fulfill in the wild—to cover the soil.

Essentially, ground covers are low-growing plants that spread by underground stems or are by nature of trailing habit. As they grow and develop, they form mats or carpets on the surface of the soil. Some produce roots along their stems, which serve to keep them flat and hold soil. Others spread by trailing stems in a procumbent manner so as to create a slightly wavy, or billowy, effect, without forming roots unless induced. The manner in which these plants develop roots and the depth to which they penetrate the soil determine their value as soil binders.

Gardening with ground covers is gardening with Nature in another sense. When we cover the soil in our gardens with carpet plants, we provide the natural environment for the breakdown of vegetable material. Not all the seeds and leaves and flower pods and stems that fall on the ground are returned to the soil. Very often, in gardens, they are raked up and burned in our attempt to keep the place tidy, but this is not Nature's way. The most practical and easy approach to soil building is to allow the growth that came out of the soil to return to it. Ground covers do precisely that kind of service, for they catch these materials as they fall and provide the conditions needed for their breakdown.

When we realize that it has taken eons of time to produce the soil in which we grow plants, and when we consider how thoughtless we are with regard to its conservation and buildup, we can take heart as we plant ground covers. These plants—used in shrub borders, under trees, among perennials, and for carpeting where grass cannot be used, or on slopes and banks to check erosion—make possible a long-range buildup of humus or organic matter, so essential to good growth.

As twigs and leaves and stems fall from nearby trees and shrubs and are deposited among the ground covers that clothe the ground, they tend to deteriorate. This deterioration, in its gradual breakdown, is the primary source of humus. Then, too, as ground covers grow and develop, they shed leaves, stems, flowers, and seed pods which are returned to the earth to renew it with that most precious of all substances in the soil—organic matter. Likewise, the flowering bulbs and temporary plants set in groups among the ground covers return in their own way to the soil from which they sprang.

Bunchberry grows luxuriantly along the slopes of the New England mountains.

By growing plants in our garden we are, in most cases, providing unnatural conditions for them. Cultivating around them, digging deeply, we often disturb their roots in our attempt to improve the appearance of the soil. At the same time there are the problems of loss of moisture and the continual plague of weeds. Thus, the use of low-growing plants which mat and make carpets reduces the need for weeding and cultivation.

Making a pleasing picture on the home grounds involves not only choosing colors wisely, but also varying the shades of green. This is where ground covers come into play because of their varied textures and subtle blending possibilities. Furthermore, the use of ground covers is often the only answer for difficult areas such as slopes and spaces that are not easy to weed—areas under shrubs, between buildings, narrow strips along walks, and the like.

Some gardeners have the notion that, once ground covers are planted, all weeding is at an end. This is hardly true. In fact, the point should be made that ground covers do make gardening easier but they do *not* eliminate maintenance, by any means. For example, when young plants of pachysandra or myrtle or ivy are set out, or such plants as achillea or ajuga or any of the other perennials like lilies-of-the-valley, hostas, violets, and thyme are first planted, they still need to be weeded. However, the use of mulches can reduce greatly the time required for this chore. But weeding is not eliminated entirely when ground covers are planted, and this fact should be borne in mind.

Another factor to consider in planting ground covers is that seeds of shrubs and trees have a habit of finding their way down into moist areas around these plants and germinating. This can be an advantage or a disadvantage, depending on the plant that seeds. If it is a weed tree, these seedlings will need to be pulled out as they appear. Otherwise, your grounds will soon develop into a young forest. On the other hand, if the seedling is of a desirable kind, it can be transplanted to a suitable place on the grounds.

In many present-day gardens there is more bare soil than is desirable to look at or practical to maintain. Bare ground means that frequent weeding or mulching or maintenance of a dust mulch is essential. It also means that, as the sun bakes the soil, it tends to rob it of some of the needed organic matter. From an aesthetic standpoint, bare ground is much less appealing than soil carpeted with green.

Ground supporting green growth is protected from the harsh rays of the sun and thus is looser and more readily able to absorb moisture

Erigerons and other wildings meet the sea at Carmel, California.

when it rains or the area is watered. Likewise, ground covers shade soil and prevent evaporation.

From the practical standpoint, ground covers are often as important as grass in the control of dust and mud near entrances and in various areas throughout the garden. Another point to remember is that ground covers used in plantings and areas close to wooden buildings absorb water from dripping eaves and protect the painted surfaces from being spattered during rain.

Ground-cover plants include those miniature types which cling to the soil and grow less than 1 inch high for use between and around stepping stones, on terraces and patios, and in other areas where a flat mass can be used as a substitute for grass to cover the soil and soften the appearance of paved areas. In this respect, there are a number of perennial matting plants, some of which are more permanent and more satisfactory than others.

Not all ground covers are plants of equal worth and merit. They need to be evaluated for specific use in any particular garden, not only as to texture, habit of growth, and soil requirements, but also as to over-all effect and permanence.

The approach to easier landscaping with ground covers lies in the selection of *the right plant for the right place.* There is no garden without some maintenance, and planting what will grow in difficult areas, in difficult soils, in difficult weather, and in generally difficult exposure, is the answer to making gardens and gardening easier. Finding the plants that fit the place and then meeting their requirements is, in essence, what takes the drudgery out of gardening. Plants are like people—put them in the right place and they thrive.

In addition to serving the purposes for which they are intended, many ground covers have added value for the flower arranger who enjoys using unusual foliage or small pieces of evergreens or deciduous material in miniature arrangements or for accent in larger compositions. Sprays of cotoneaster; branches of dwarf yew; snippets of ivy, myrtle, and pachysandra; clippings from the various gray-foliaged herbs, and, in fact, any of the low-growing plants that last when cut, serve to provide this desirable material. In the making of miniature arrangements and small bouquets, the flowers and fruits of many ground covers also have great value. Some of these can also be cut and dried and sprayed with silver or gold for indoor holiday decorations.

2

Landscaping with Ground Covers

Aside from their aesthetic value, ground covers fill a multitude of practical needs on the home grounds. They reduce the need for frequent watering, spraying, and feeding. Since they are shrubs, or vines, or perennials, they are plants for permanent effects. The extensive list covered in these pages includes types to solve planting problems concerned with sun and shade, various types of soil, flat surfaces and slopes, and those difficult places where grass or other plants are not well suited or do not fit. Nearly every garden has such problem areas.

Grass has been called the finest of all ground covers, a fact which few of us would dispute. Yet, there are places where grass does not grow easily and where it cannot be cared for satisfactorily. Then, too, the time required and the cost involved to maintain a high-grade lawn are often considerable. The need for continuous fertilizing, spraying for insects and pests, and frequent cutting can add up, in terms of both man-hours and dollars, to a sizable total. Furthermore, in shady areas where gardeners often struggle to keep grass growing, they spend much more time and energy than the plot is worth. The answer is ground covers.

Cover for bare soil in all parts of the garden is the primary purpose of ground covers. When not covered with grass, exposed ground needs to be planted, if only to keep it from becoming infested with weeds. These adaptable plants fulfill a variety of related needs on the home grounds, in which their practical value is easily recognized. The following are typical situations.

Concealing Exposed Tree Roots. This problem often plagues gardeners, especially if large trees are a part of or adjoin a lawn area. Grass is neither easy to cut nor easy to maintain. Exposed roots are a hazard. Cover plants solve both problems.

Carpeting Shady Areas under Trees and Shrubs. Matting plants or taller kinds are needed for soil cover, as well as to provide a pleasing setting for the trees or shrubs.

Clothing Rocky Uneven Land. Where the roughness is desired but needs cover, outcroppings of rock can become a distinctive feature of the grounds when planted with a variety of ground-cover, crevice, and rock plants.

Covering Slopes and Banks. Erosion is the chief problem in both sun and shade. Most slopes and banks are not suited to grass from the point of easy maintenance. Steep grades often require deep-rooted low-growing plants to hold the soil and to tie them in with the over-all planting scheme.

Underplanting Trees and Shrubs to Keep Down Weeds. Soil under high-branching kinds can be a nuisance to keep attractive unless some suitable cover is provided.

Providing Settings for Lilies and Other Bulbous Plants. Lilies grow best when they have shade over their roots. The contrasting foliage of ground-cover plants provides a setting and acts besides as a foil for the lilies and other kinds of flowering bulbs.

Reducing Weeds Among Perennials. This practice has proved to be most satisfactory where large-scale perennials such as peonies, hardy asters, chrysanthemums, poppies, iris, daylilies, and the like are grown.

Binding Sandy Soils. Plants that tolerate salt spray—like bearberry, rugosa roses, shore juniper, beach wormwood, and many others—are invaluable for holding soil in seaside plantings and sandy soils inland.

Solving Problems in Wet Soils. Some creeping plants are by nature adapted to boggy conditions where they thrive on hummocks. Others prefer moist, heavy soil.

Ground covers in their diverse forms lend a finished appearance to shrub and perennial plantings, thereby eliminating sharp edges between beds and grass areas. Large surfaces of bare ground are not particularly pleasing, since the soil tends to cake and crust. Unless the beds are mulched with peat moss or some other suitable material, or a

(*Above*) Heather, cotoneasters, lavender, and pachysandra provide a variety of texture.

(*Below*) Myrtle makes green carpets under trees.

dust mulch is maintained, weeds appear which require cultivation to eradicate. A good-looking mat of green is preferable to a weedy tangle between clumps of perennials or groups of shrubs.

These versatile creepers have value in the over-all landscape picture for linking the various units of a planting on the home grounds, so that one flows into the other. The transition between a lawn and the trees and shrubs that enclose it can be enhanced by the use of a medium-sized cover. Small shrub groupings can also be softened with ground covers. Plants of varying sizes and shapes within a unit can be linked or tied together with one or more kinds of carpet plants. This is particularly true in foundation plantings.

Evergreen ground covers are especially valuable for their year-round color and interest. They become eye-catchers in plantings that can be viewed from windows, driveways, and roads adjoining one's property. They are equally important in approach plantings, corner group- ings, strips along walks, and other areas adjacent to the house—be it the front door, the service entrance, or the rear driveway. Blankets or sheets of cover plants are the simple and easy solution to tasteful landscaping. They seem to belong in these locations.

Settings for garden ornaments (such as pools, figures, and benches) can often be softened and appreciably improved with a low ground cover. For example, English ivy, periwinkle, Christmas fern, or any number of others break the sharp outline of a shady pool. These same plants and others make light tracery against the base of a pedestal on which a figure is placed. Similar effects can be developed at the bases of bird baths, sundials, and other decorative objects. All too often, the ground under a garden bench is completely forgotten and soon becomes a spot where weeds get a hold. How much better to establish some carpeting plant that will make it look as though it belonged there.

Contemporary architecture frequently calls for tailored planting. In contrast to the era of houses with high foundations when basement walls were. exposed, the present-day house is low-slung and fits into the landscape. Where slight or severe changes of grade occur, broad masses of low-growing plants may be all that are needed. Medium or tall-growing ground covers can be utilized to good advantage in these situations. Very often an evergreen shrub such as a dwarf yew gives the desired result when grouped in broad masses. (See Chapter 7 for other suggestions.)

Changes of level on the home grounds are often a challenge that can be solved with cover plants. Instead of a grassy bank, the area

(*Above*) Low-growing junipers fit well in this contemporary setting.

(*Below*) A flag terrace becomes a fascinating garden.

can be planted with spreading junipers, dwarf cotoneasters, or other low-growing shrubs. This kind of treatment can be a refreshing change, since it relieves monotony and reduces the abruptness of a steep grade.

Ground covers to soften the edges of steps and paths and make them blend with the surrounding landscape have their place in the garden. The spaces between steps, the crevices on terraces and other flat-stoned paving areas, are greatly enhanced by such alpine ground covers as moss sandwort, thyme, creeping speedwell, and other equally adaptable kinds.

Tall-growing perennials often have bare legs, or shoddy-looking stems. These can be concealed with such ground covers as candytuft, pachistima, coral bells, lady's-mantle, plantain-lilies, and others.

The service area on the home property often has nooks and corners or narrow strips where there is no room for shrubs. These are other locations where ground covers can take over.

Formal treatment of ground surfaces (as illustrated in this chapter) can be carried out most effectively with ground covers, either in distinct patterns or in a combination of several kinds. There is also the possibility of decorative textured effects with pebbles, stones, or crushed rock spread as a mulch under these plants.

Ground covers make a charming underplanting in a city garden.

3

Gardening with Green

Ground covers play many roles in present-day landscaping. Gardening with them, to any extent, means gardening with green, for it is foliage in all its variations of color that is the enduring element with cover plants. Flowers, at best, are of fleeting beauty, but it is the quality, the texture, and particularly the endurance of the foliage that counts.

Green is the result of blending yellow and blue. When yellow is the predominant pigment, the effect is a warm green. On the other hand, when blue is the stronger component, the result is a cool hue. In its full intensity, green is vibrant and refreshing and ever-pleasing. It becomes monotonous only when there are no contrasts, and seldom is this condition found in Nature. When it prevails in gardens it is due to lack of thoughtful selection of plant materials.

The rich and subtle tonal effects of green are all the more apparent in the blue-green, gray-green, yellow-green, olive and bottle-green we see all about us. Leaf surfaces, shiny or dull, woolly or smooth, are often crinkled or wavy, conspicuously veined or ribbed. Overtones of gray, bronze, gold, silver, red, purple, and other colors in softer value add further to the fascination of green. There's more to green than often meets the eye at first glance.

Plants valued primarily for their foliage give us a new awareness of green and its significance. The dominant color in Nature (and the

most restful of all colors to the eye), green changes from hour to hour, its variations being more apparent at some seasons of the year than others. In winter, the dormant time of year, its value is heightened. If ground covers have been grouped tastefully, the leaf pattern and the texture of the foliage stand out all the more conspicuously at this barren season.

The size and the pattern of foliage play a dominant part in Nature's eternal symphony of green. A variety of forms well blended, such as found in Nature, makes the richest kind of tapestried effect. Small-leaved evergreens like myrtle and bearberry on trailing stems used in long irregular drifts or sheets give a flowing effect. Masses of large leaves well placed are like staccato notes: they arrest the eye and give emphasis to a planting or to a unit in the over-all design. Finely cut foliage like that of ferns has a subtle quality, adding needed height without bulkiness.

Slopes and banks and areas where there are slight changes of level need not be monotonous with one kind of green. By selecting low-growing, needle-like, blue-green evergreens (such as junipers), and interplanting them with the small-leaved, rounded, dark green foliage of the creeping cotoneasters or some other plants of contrasting tone and texture, you can achieve a marked contrast which is pleasing to the eye and relieves the monotony resulting from the use of a solid mass of one type of leaf.

This practice is also adaptable in areas flanking steps connecting one level of the garden with the other. These approaches are softened and appear shortened in height by using plants of varying types of foliage and varying height. Slight slopes in shade or sun where grass is neither practical nor desirable become showcases for matting or carpeting plants. Viewed from an angle, the play of light accentuates their texture and adds considerable interest to the over-all picture. Working with green in its endless variety of tonal values is every bit as exciting as creating effects with the brighter colors—indeed, it is even more challenging to the imagination.

Just as painters use drapery in a composition to create the feeling of movement, so gardeners can adapt these flowing lines to planting design for similar effects. Cover plants used as carpets and blankets in casual drifts or in wide streamers over the surfaces of the soil—particularly where there are changes of level or the ground is naturally

← **The play of light and shadow on periwinkle.**

sloping—create that pleasing kind of flowing effect that links together all parts of the home grounds.

Using green carpets this way gives the taller perennials, the trees, and the shrubs the kind of anchorage they need to fit into the picture. Furthermore, the use of curved lines in the making of wide border plantings with ground covers helps to lead the eye toward some point of interest and creates a feeling of spaciousness, even on a small lot.

The play of light and shadow on drifts of green is important in gardens large and small. When a mass of bold foliage is highlighted by sun streaming through overhead trees—dappled light, we call it— plants in the shadow seem all the richer in their texture. Thus, a kind of magic is created. It plays tricks with our eyes as it spotlights the foliage in its path and lends a note of glamour to the setting.

In full sun, effects equally pleasing are created with drifts of silvery foliage of gray-leaved plants used for contrast with masses of green. The more we work with plants, the more we realize how these subtle and easy-to-achieve effects add tone and style to home grounds, particularly during the hot summer months. The effect of these gray-leaved plants is equally bright on a dull day.

Ivy, periwinkle, and Christmas ferns flourish where grass would be impractical.

4

A Selection of Ground Covers

The selection of ground covers in this chapter includes perennials, vines, dwarf shrubs, and a number of plants generally associated with rock gardens. It also includes sub-shrubs, an important group of ground covers, which are partly woody, such as pachysandra and artemisia. They have been chosen for their natural trailing habit of growth; their method of increase by underground stems, stolons, rootstocks, or rhizomes; and their tendency to produce carpet-like growth of varying heights when planted in masses. The quality of their foliage, whether evergreen or deciduous, has also been a prime factor for inclusion, since the substance and the durability of the leaves of carpeting plants are their chief assets for use as ground covers.

Since this book has been written primarily for amateur gardeners, the plants are purposely listed alphabetically by their common, most generally accepted, names. Many of these are more familiar to amateurs than their scientific names. However, the botanical names appear on the same line. Easy reference to the Index will permit you quickly to locate every plant included, listed under both its common and its technical names.

The height designated includes the total normal growth of foliage and blooms. In many cases the foliage mass is considerably lower, and this point is usually indicated in the description.

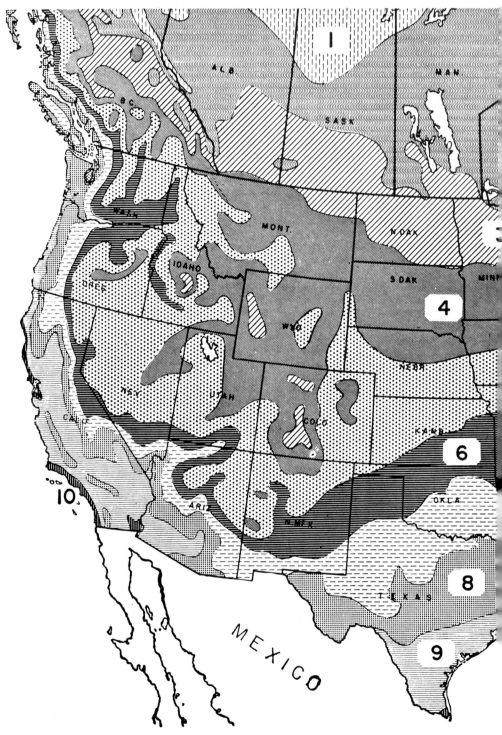

Hardiness Zones—United States and Canada (Revised by USDA 1960)

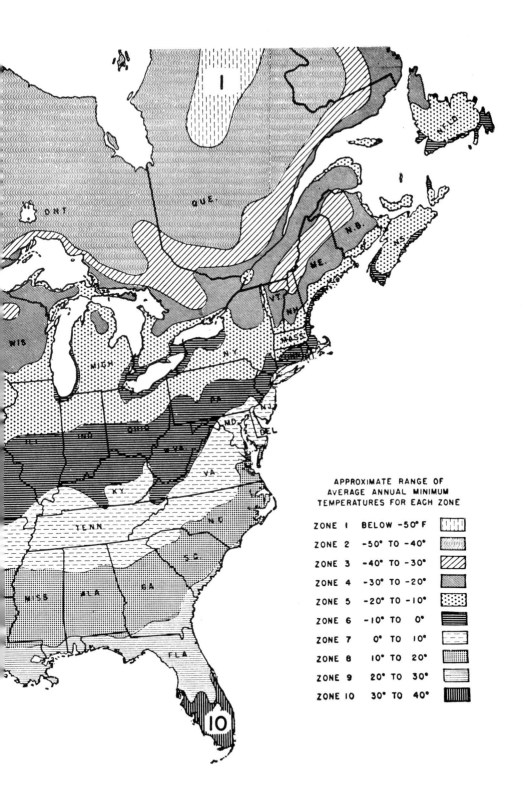

APPROXIMATE RANGE OF
AVERAGE ANNUAL MINIMUM
TEMPERATURES FOR EACH ZONE

ZONE 1	BELOW -50° F	
ZONE 2	-50° TO -40°	
ZONE 3	-40° TO -30°	
ZONE 4	-30° TO -20°	
ZONE 5	-20° TO -10°	
ZONE 6	-10° TO 0°	
ZONE 7	0° TO 10°	
ZONE 8	10° TO 20°	
ZONE 9	20° TO 30°	
ZONE 10	30° TO 40°	

Hardiness is indicated on the basis of the "Zone Map of Plant Hardiness," revised in 1960 by the United States Department of Agriculture. In some instances the plants discussed have proved to be hardy in selected areas north of the zone indicated. It is practically impossible, however, to designate precise limits for some kinds of uncertain hardiness, because of the environmental factors involved.

All the plants listed in this chapter are available in the trade at the present time, but some may not be obtainable as readily as others. Often plants are sold under a variety of names, including those no longer considered valid by plant scientists. The fact that plant names are not completely stabilized sometimes leads to confusion, but, generally speaking, this problem is not too difficult to overcome.

In order not to make this general listing unwieldy, a number of plants widely adapted as ground covers for limited or special types of use are discussed in Chapters 6 and 7. Ferns are presented in Chapter 5 and annuals for temporary effects in Chapter 8.

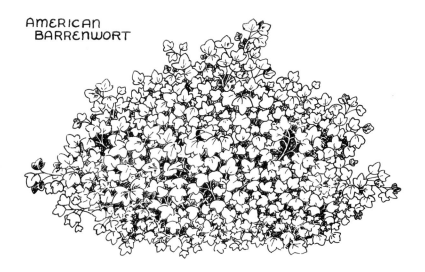

AMERICAN
BARRENWORT

American Barrenwort—15"—Zone 5   *Vancouveria*

Little known to most gardeners, vancouveria is a perennial native to the Northwest; it serves as an interesting shady-ground cover. Combined with ferns and epimedium, it creates an effect that is a pleasant change from some of the coarser ground covers. White flowers in panicles in late spring and leathery foliage are its chief assets.

Essentially a shade-loving plant, it grows best in good garden soil. Stock is increased by division.

Aubrieta—8"—Zone 3   *Aubrieta deltoidea*

This neat-growing rock plant, which flowers with arabis, moss pink, and other spring alpines, makes dense mats of warm gray foliage with masses of bloom ranging from mauve to deep purple. It creeps over rocks and seems to be at home wherever it can root itself in stony crevices. In combination with arabis and other alpines of similar habit, it is most desirable for rocky areas and gritty soil, especially on slight slopes.

Easily raised from seed, which produces great variety in color, it can also be divided after flowering. Shearing and occasional feeding keep the plants thrifty. Well-drained, gritty soil and a slight slope in the sun are its needs.

Aubrieta makes a colorful mound of bloom above gray foliage.

Baby-Tears—Zone 7   *Helxine soleiroli*

A moss-like plant seen as a carpet under greenhouse benches or as a house plant, this can serve as a temporary ground cover in the coldest sections of the Northeast. In the warmer sections of the country it is used like moss to make a dense mat under larger plants, among ferns, or in shady moist places around pools. Delicate and soft in texture, it gives a finished appearance to bare ground. The scientific name is not easy to pronounce, but most people know it as baby- or angel-tears.

Moist soil suits it best and the smallest piece will make a new plant. It spreads rapidly.

Barrenwort—6–9″—Zone 3   *Epimedium species*

Barrenwort and bishop's-hat are two common names for one of the most satisfactory of all perennial ground covers, a member of the barberry family called *Epimedium*. Its common country name, bishop's-hat, known to most gardeners, refers to the curious shape of the

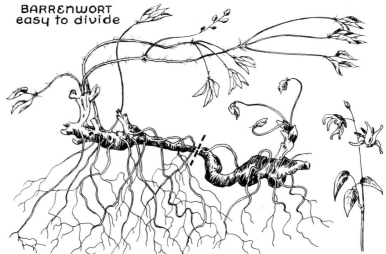

BARRENWORT
easy to divide

blossom, which resembles a biretta. A charming blossom for small arrangements, it lasts well as a cut flower and the foliage has many uses at various seasons of the year. For colonizing under spring-flowering shrubs and trees, in combination with other early-flowering ground covers or in broad masses by itself, it is always pleasing. It can be used in front of the taller-growing Vancouveria, to which it is related. This Japanese native spreads by creeping rhizomes, making a tightly entwined mass of roots and foliage when well established.

E. grandiflorum, which is most commonly grown, has heart-shaped leaves suspended on stiff, wiry stems. Red tones show in the new foliage

Barrenwort is noted for its dainty flowers and distinctive foliage.

in spring and bronzy-red coloring enhances its appearance in autumn, lasting into winter and even into a second spring where winters are mild. The delicately formed, spurred flowers which appear in loose sprays during May may be white, yellow, pink, or violet, according to variety. *E. alpinum rubrum* is more dwarf in habit, with compound leaves and rich red blooms. Bright yellow flowers with red for contrast are typical of *E. pinnatum*. A number of hybrid forms appear under various names.

The better the soil in humus content, the better the growth of this little charmer. It thrives in acid soil, which can be improved with peat moss and leafmold. Shady locations are preferable where summers are hot, but it does well in sun where soil is deep and moist. Easy to increase by division after flowering or in early fall, heavy clumps may need to be cut apart with a sharp knife. Since it is reliably hardy and easy to grow, most gardeners never have enough of it.

Beach Wormwood—18–24″—Zone 2 *Artemisia stelleriana*

Silvery-gray and almost white in the bright sunlight, this creeping perennial of the sand dunes, commonly known by several names, is often called dusty miller. The leaves, like those of a small oak, are soft and silky and look as though they were cut from fine cloth. It spreads by creeping stems and thrives in hot, dry, sandy soils. Heavy wet soil will finish it in short order. Tolerant of salt spray and rugged, it makes an ideal cover for seaside gardens. Used with dwarf forms of *Rosa rugosa,* it makes a striking contrast. Or it may be blended with the strap-like foliage of daylilies, the coarse olive-green of bayberries, or the needle-like foliage of the shore juniper and the dark green cut-leaved sweet fern. (For other artemisias, see Silver Mound Artemisia.)

Propagated by root division or by cuttings, it requires little or no care except a hot, dry location and light soil of poor quality. To thicken the growth, cut it back in early spring.

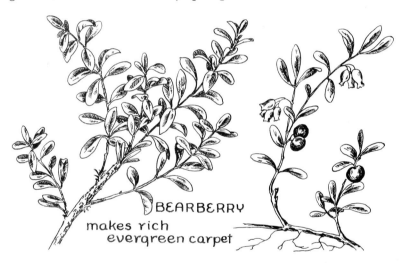

BEARBERRY makes rich evergreen carpet

Bearberry—12″—Zone 2 *Arctostaphylos Uva-ursi*
Hooker Manzanita—18″—Zone 7 *A. hookeri*
Laurel Hill Manzanita—6″—Zone 7 *A. franciscana*

Bearberry, or kinnikinnick, as the Indians called it, is a trailing evergreen shrub widely distributed over a large part of the United States. It is at home in dry, sandy, or rocky acid soil, where it makes long, trailing mats of rich, leathery foliage showing bronzy tones in autumn. The white bell-shaped flowers, borne in clusters on dark red stems during May and June, are followed by red fruits in autumn. An ideal ground cover and binder for sunny banks and slopes in hot,

Bearberry makes a broad-spreading mat for hot, dry places.

dry, sandy locations, it is being widely used throughout the country in gardens and along highways both near the sea and inland.

Other species native to the West Coast, commonly referred to as manzanitas (little apples), range from small trailing forms to small trees. These are the most familiar shrubs of the California chaparral belt, hardy from Zone 7 southward. To the California Indians, the fruits were considered the little apples of God, since they furnished an important source of food in the form of a dried meal served as porridge. Laurel Hill manzanita (*A. franciscana*) has gray-green foliage, grows about 6 inches high, and creeps at a rapid rate. Hooker manzanita (*A. hookeri*) is taller-growing, 18 inches to 2 feet in height, and makes a neat mound of shiny foliage several yards wide. Both have pink flowers in early spring, followed by "little apples." These plants layer naturally as they creep. For sandy banks and slopes and general ground-cover use on the West Coast, these native plants are of prime importance and value.

For success in planting, the bearberry and the manzanita must be handled with care because of the sensitive root systems. Prepare the area for use with a mixture of acid peat moss and sandy loam and use nursery-grown stock from containers. Few gardeners are ever successful in transplanting them from the wild unless they are carefully handled in large mats or clumps and moved with their native soil. This method of handling is best done in early spring; some gardeners have been known to move sods of bearberry before the frost has left the soil. Frequent watering, shading from wind, and mulching are necessary to establish these plants in exposed areas, but it is worth the effort involved. However, nurserymen who propagate them from cuttings offer small potted or container-grown plants which are easy to handle throughout the growing season. Two- or three-year rooted cuttings are not impressive in appearance, but once established they make fairly rapid growth.

Bedstraw—2'—Zone 3 *Galium verum*

Yellow or Lady's-bedstraw is a European weed which is sometimes equally weedy in America, where it has been naturalized. Herb gardeners grow it sometimes as a coarse ground cover. Its common name, Our Lady's-bedstraw, connects it with the tradition that this plant was part of the straw in the manger at Bethlehem. Where is there a gardener who is not attracted by such lore? Usually somewhat loose and untidy, it can be kept in hand by shearing. Tiny yellow flowers arranged in whorls of leathery foliage appear in early summer.

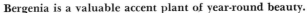

Bergenia is a valuable accent plant of year-round beauty.

This is a plant for poor soil in full sun. When grown in much shade it becomes untidy. Root division is the easiest method of increase.

Bergenia—1′—Zone 4   *Bergenia cordifolia*

Bergenia is one of those fairly well-known perennials seldom used to best advantage. Landscape designers enjoy using it as an accent plant for colonizing in the crevices of large rocks or in a sizable mass with small-leaved ground covers in sun or shade for contrast. Striking in appearance when well placed, its leathery leaves resemble those of a water lily and stand erect, often at interesting angles. Actually, there is more to gardening with ground covers than the mere planting of carpet plants, and we need to work with them as with shrubs and trees.

Amazingly hardy, since it is native to Siberia, it creeps by underground rootstocks. It is sometimes listed as a saxifrage or under the name megasea. The sturdy flower spikes on 8-inch stems, topped with rounded heads of pink flowers, appear early in the spring. There are also white and purple forms. Siberian tea (*B. crassifolia*), which resembles it somewhat, has similar possibilities.

Give it a well-drained situation in ordinary soil. It is equally adaptable in sun or part shade. Propagation is by division of the rootstock.

Bird's-Foot Trefoil—6–12″—Zone 4   *Lotus corniculatus*

Ground honeysuckle, baby's-slippers, bloom-fell, and some 70 other local common names are associated with this perennial with yellow pea-like flowers and dainty foliage. Its prime use is on slopes and banks along some of our major highways, where it endures drought, heat, and poor soil, and can be sheared besides. In gardens with good soil it becomes a rather lush, low shrub and is listed as one of the noxious lawn weeds.

It is increased by seed for highway plantings, but roots can be divided or cuttings made.

Bloodroot—10″—Zone 2   *Sanguinaria canadensis*

Beautiful and fragile though the flowers are, the sturdy roots and the durable foliage of bloodroot make it one of the most satisfactory of wildings to tame in gardens. It is one of the earliest plants to bloom in spring; the white petals with showy yellow centers are of passing moment, but so very welcome when they appear. Of more lasting value is the double form, with clusters of shapely blooms that look like miniature peonies or small double water lilies. This is a hybrid found in the wild which has become popular on both sides of the Atlantic.

(*Top*) Bloodroot is happiest in partial shade.

(*Bottom*) Double bloodroot is one of the most sought-after of native wildings.

As a foreground planting for ferns or mingled with other wild flowers, bloodroot with its handsome blue-green leaves, curiously lobed and scalloped, makes a ribbon of pleasing texture, but the foliage disappears in late summer. Keep it free of vigorous trailing evergreens such as myrtle, for it must not be smothered. It increases by thick creeping rootstocks of bright orange color, somewhat resembling the rhizomes of iris.

Give it rich, moist soil with ample humus and a shady location. Increase your stock by dividing the rootstocks in fall, covering them with 1 inch of soil. Once established, it self-sows, scattering seedlings in a casual manner.

Blue Fescue—6–8″—Zone 3   *Festuca ovina glauca*

This blue-gray grass is a fascinating plant that grows in tufts, making a striking appearance when it is used to make a patterned ground cover. The name fescue brings to mind other kinds of grasses well suited to shade, and all of them have this characteristic of growing in tufts or bunches, but none so pronounced as the blue fescue. It must have perfect drainage and dry soil. It had a vogue among rock-garden enthusiasts some 20 years ago, but it is not widely known in the Northeast. West Coast gardeners use it in block plantings alternating with brick patterns, using various plants in masses with it for contrast and also as a ground cover under trees.

Easy to increase by dividing the clumps, it benefits from occasional shearing. It takes heat and plenty of it, but will grow in light shade.

Blue Leadwort—6–12″—Zone 5   *Ceratostigma plumbaginoides*

Summer-flowering ground covers are few in number. Blue leadwort, a native of China, often used in large rock gardens, makes a vigorous carpet of oval foliage of even height which shows warm bronze tones in autumn. Partially evergreen in mild climates, it suckers readily, making a solid mat, but it is slow to start growth in spring. An underplanting for shrubs, it can be used successfully on slopes and banks. The heads of deep blue flowers, carried on wiry stems in late summer, are as rich as any gentian and also enduring, continuing until late fall. It is listed in many catalogs as *Plumbago Larpentiae*.

This is a vigorous grower for sun or part shade, growing in ordinary garden soil. The tiniest rooted division will make a new plant and early spring is the easiest time to handle it. It can become weedy once established, for it is a rapid grower, but it serves well as a ground cover. In areas where the winters are severe, it loses its evergreen character—a fact to bear in mind when planting it.

Bluets—4–6"—Zone 1   *Houstonia caerulea*

This familiar spring flower makes broad carpets of growth in moist woodlands, often around rocks. It sends forth its tiny blue flowers, marked with yellow eyes, from creeping evergreen foliage in April and May. Best suited to shady places along walks or between stones, it is a ground cover for limited use in acid soil, with great charm and appeal. It is sometimes found with partridge berry and wintergreen. The star violet or thyme-leaf bluet, as it is occasionally called, (*H. serpyllifolia*) spreads by creeping stems and is a deeper blue with slightly taller stems.

Both kinds are best increased by root division, and if given moist, woodsy soil in light shade will increase readily.

Pink Spire bugleweed is one of the showiest of the tribe.

Variegated bugleweed makes bright drifts in dark places.

Bugleweed—4–12″—Zone 4   *Ajuga species*

Bugleweed and carpet bugle are rather meaningless names for a low-growing perennial which has become one of our leading ground covers in recent years. The term bugle probably refers to a long tube-shaped bead sewn on women's clothes, an ornament the flower somewhat resembles. In the Austrian countryside, it is known as blue steeple, which vividly describes the showy flower spikes. Old garden writers mention it frequently and it has a dozen or more picturesque local names. One of them, carpenter's herb, refers to its use as an herb for wounds.

Few perennial ground covers do a better job of quick covering and are easier to handle and increase in gardens than bugleweed. It is widely used in shade as a substitute for grass, both on flat areas and on slopes. For carpeting under shrubs and trees, in strip plantings, among rocks, on terraces, or between stone crevices, it is one of the easiest of all ground covers to grow. The blue, pink, and white forms grouped together make a colorful display. However, it does not stand any great amount of foot traffic. Except in naturally dry soils, this plant flourishes with little care. It is ideal for shade or partial shade, or in sunny locations where there is more than average soil moisture.

Common bugle (*A. reptans*) is the most rapid grower of all. The rosettes of glossy foliage lie flat on the ground and it spreads by creeping stems from 3 to 10 inches or more in length. Some kinds do not produce runners, and their ability to cover is not so rapid. Sturdy, upright flower spikes, 3 to 6 inches tall, bloom in May and June. Blue is the predominant color, but there are pink- and white-flowering kinds and several have bronze, variegated, or mottled foliage. Many kinds are listed by growers because of the great demand for this plant. Some are selections of recognized forms and others are of hybrid origin. The following list of species and varieties probably contains some duplicates, but this is the way they are sold.

Ajuga reptans. Common Bugle.
> *alba.* Light green foliage and white flowers.
> *atropurpurea.* Bronze leaves with blue spikes.
> *Bronze Beauty.* A selection with large bronzy-and-blue flowers.
> *multicolor.* Spotted and variegated yellow, brown, and red with blue flowers.
> *Rainbow.* Similar to multicolor and may be identical.
> *Silver Beauty.* Green-and-white foliage, not a rampant grower.
> *variegata conspicua.* Creamy-white markings and blue flowers.

A. genevensis. Geneva or Alpine Bugle. This species tends to make broad mats, does not spread so rapidly, being without runners.
> *brockbanki.* Dwarf habit, with deep blue flower spikes.
> *metallica crispa.* Dark bronze foliage with a metallic quality, crisped edges, blue flowers.
> *Rosy Spires.* Bright green foliage with showy pink flowers.

A. pyramidalis. An improved form with bottle-green foliage and larger flower spikes than those listed above.

Easy to increase, the smallest piece with roots will take hold. It can be set out at any time during the growing season, since it requires only ordinary soil and routine care in transplanting. Ground covers for shade are not too numerous, and this is one of the most useful and least expensive because of its rapid method of increase. Ajuga has a shallow rooting system and shows the effects of prolonged dry spells in thin soils, but responds quickly to watering.

Bunchberry naturalized in a shady city garden with seedling firs.

Bunchberry—9"—Zone 2   *Cornus canadensis*

Where is there a native ground cover that can compare with the bunchberry? A plant of arresting beauty, it is found in high altitudes, in cool, moist woods, and on hummocks in bogs. Its natural range extends from Greenland south to the mountains of West Virginia and west to Minnesota, Colorado, and California. In his delightful book, "American Wild Flowers," Harold L. Moldenke reminds us that its setting is often a "sylvan glen of paper or gray birch, richly carpeted with soft ground pine, delicate twinflower, Clintonia, partridge-berry, goldthread, many kinds of ferns and here and there groups of the lovely bunchberry."

Bunchberry is notable for its showy white bracts, its bright scarlet berries, its luxuriant foliage, its dwarf form, and its carpeting habit. The true flowers are inconspicuous greenish-white, borne in a tight cluster like a button, but it is the showy white bracts surrounding them that give the plant its appeal. These appear from May to July, depending on the elevation at which it is grown. In late summer, clusters of scarlet fruits nestle in the centers of the rosettes of yellow-green foliage. These remain to add richness to the foliage until eaten by the birds.

Not everyone succeeds in establishing the bunchberry or dwarf cornel, and part of the problem lies in not meeting the soil requirements. It needs a moist, acid soil rich in organic matter. Equally important is a cool atmosphere such as that found at high elevations or near the sea. On wooded properties where it can have these conditions or they can be met by watering in dry summers, it is well worth growing. Once it is acclimated, there are few native ground covers which make a handsomer, denser carpet of green in high shade, under evergreens, or where there is a leafy canopy overhead.

Sods cut from established plantings and placed in well-prepared soil make the easiest method of establishing it. These need frequent watering until well established. A mulch of acid peat moss or pine needles helps to conserve soil moisture.

Camomile—3–6″—Zone 3   *Anthemis nobilis*

This ancient carpeting plant, used as a lawn substitute in the gardens of Europe since the Middle Ages, has from time to time come up for discussion and experimental use. The finely cut, bright green foliage is most attractive and emits a pleasing fragrance when stepped upon. Since it becomes irregular and unkempt with age, it requires mowing or shearing. The typical form of this plant produces a small daisy-like flower on stems to 1 foot high and is a familiar naturalized weed in many parts of the United States. Formerly used to make a vile-tasting tea and also as a hair rinse "to keep blondes blonde," this plant came to America with the early settlers.

The camomile cultivated for lawns is a variety whose flowers have no ray petals—only yellow, button-like centers. It has been used somewhat on the West Coast. A form similar to the turfing daisy (*Matricaria tchihatchewi*), is taller-growing, to about 6 inches, and is coarser in texture.

It can be sown broadcast like lawn seed or in a seed bed from which plants are set out 6 inches apart, like plugs of certain grasses. It needs full sun, but will take light shade. Mowing or shearing is needed as plants develop, and it requires rolling to keep the surface flat. It is no plant for cold, windswept areas or areas where summer winds dry it out. Heavy traffic is sure to create worn spots, and the best that can be said is that it is a questionable substitute for grass, except in moist climates, and requires considerable care.

Cinquefoil—6″–3′—Zone 2   *Potentilla species*

These are considered weedy plants, commonly found in many parts of the world. The leaves of some look like the five fingers of a hand, hence the common name, but not all are five-parted. A number of kinds resemble the foliage of strawberries, to which they are related. Flowers resemble those of strawberries but have a wide color range. Except for the kinds grown in rock gardens, they had been ignored by gardeners until several shrubby forms appeared in glowing color in nursery catalogs a few years ago. The cinquefoils thrive in hot, dry situations, have clean and attractive foliage and ironclad hardiness. As ground covers in sunny locations, they provide not only good foliage but good bloom as well.

Carpeting kinds include the wineleaf cinquefoil (*P. tridentata*), with small white flowers, strawberry-like leaves, which is at home in acid soil and full sun and makes a low, glossy mat 6 inches or more in

Cinquefoil provides an abundance of color all summer in hot, dry situations.

height. Rusty cinquefoil (*P. cinerea*), native to Europe, fits into the picture on the West Coast. *P. tommassinianus,* with small gray foliage and bright yellow flowers in May, is listed in some catalogs, as are many fascinating kinds featured by specialists in rock plants. Many of these deserve wider use as cover plants.

More imposing in appearance and in flower are two hybrids known as *Gold Drop* and *Katherine Dykes. Gold Drop* is an improved form of the shrubby cinquefoil (*P. fruticosa*), long considered a troublesome weed. Yet, this improved form, with its fern-like leaves and bright buttercup-yellow flowers which appear all summer, is a thing of beauty in hot, dry places. It makes a loose mound and can be used in masses for a colorful high-level ground cover, about 2 feet tall. *Katherine Dykes* is taller, to 3 feet, of more upright habit, and can be used for accent among low carpet plants in sunny areas or in groups in a large shrub border.

Full sun and average garden soil on the acid side are all these plants need. Increase is by division of the roots, or from cuttings for the tall forms.

Coral Bells—18″—Zone 4   *Heuchera sanguinea*

One of the most rewarding of all perennials grown in home gardens is coral bells. We think of it as a border plant with good evergreen foliage and feathery pink flowers. For sun or partial shade it makes a colorful display from early spring well into summer. As a ground cover for limited use it is highly decorative. There are many hybrid forms which are colorful and delightful, but the sturdiest of them all is *H. sanguinea.*

Coral bells grows well in ordinary well-drained garden soil and makes a good showing in partial shade, but it is at its best in full sun. Increase it by division of the roots in spring or late summer or at any time during the growing season.

Cotoneaster—1–3′—Zones 5–6   *Cotoneaster species*

In the early twenties, that intrepid plant hunter, Ernest H. Wilson, introduced nearly three dozen kinds of cotoneasters to American gardens from the Orient. He used to rejoice in the fact that there were kinds suitable for practically every section of the United States. The delicate tracery of the twigs, especially the low-growing rocksprays, and their fan-like branching habit are notable characteristics of these sprawling shrubs. When seen protruding through the snow, or viewed in the barren winter landscape with the sun glistening on the bright berries, they become all the more appealing. Often they have been planted in the wrong places and then hacked back with no thought to their form. Cotoneasters need room to develop the fullness of their beauty.

Cotoneasters are plants for hot, dry situations on banks and slopes exposed to the wind. Skirting the top or base of a wall or among rocks, where they can develop their broad-spreading habit and free-branching growth, they are particularly decorative. They are deep-rooted and make good soil binders. Combine them with the low-spreading junipers or use an occasional plant in a bank of pachysandra, since they grow well in part shade.

Rockspray cotoneaster softens a stone wall.

Cotoneasters are subject to several pests, including fire-blight, scale, lace bug, and red spider, which disfigure their appearance and defoliate the plants. Sprays for the control of all these pests are effective, but they must be applied at the proper time. Present-day gardeners have become keenly aware of pests and diseases in the past decade and these drawbacks must be faced in selecting quantities of any given plant for landscaping. Cotoneasters are no exception in this respect.

All the kinds mentioned here have white or pinkish flowers in June, followed by showy red fruits which add to the attractiveness of the plants in autumn. Best known of all is the rockspray cotoneaster (*C. horizontalis*).

Bearberry C. (*C. dammeri*): Distinctly flat in growth with evergreen foliage. The branches often root at the joints. This makes a most desirable ground cover because of its vigorous growth. Hardy from Zone 5, it is considered one of the good forms among the low-growing kinds.

Cranberry C. (*C. apiculata*): Seldom more than 18 inches tall, it has glossy leaves, sizable fruits, and flat branching habit.

Creeping C. (*C. adpressa praecox*): A compact grower, it forms mounds a little more than 1 foot high, with wavy, glossy leaves and large red berries. Its restrained habit makes it desirable for planting in formal areas where trim, even growth is desired.

Dwarf Silver-Leaf C. (*C. pannosa nana*): A Chinese native averaging 1 foot high, it is valued for its gray-green foliage and stiff horizontal growth. This species is not so hardy as most of the dwarfs and is suited to Zone 6 southward.

Necklace C. (*C. decora*): Similar in habit to *C. horizontalis* with clear red fruits; the foliage is silvery-gray.

Rockspray C. (*C. horizontalis*): Semi-evergreen in mild climates, it sheds its leaves in cold regions by early winter. The lacy twigs, red fruits, and horizontal habit of this plant make it most useful as big-scale ground or rock cover. Mature plants may grow to 3 feet high, but they usually remain a foot lower and can be controlled by pruning. Plants eventually spread 8 to 10 feet or more in width—a point to remember when planting them. Hardy for Zone 4.

Small-Leaved C. (*C. microphylla*): Small-leaved with rosy-red fruits and long cascading branches, it makes dense growth. Foliage is about half the size of *C. horizontalis*. Zone 4.

Thyme-Leaved C. (*C. microphylla thymifolia*): With narrow leaves of extremely delicate form and tiny fruits, it is a most attractive plant, compact in habit, averaging a foot in height. Hardy from Zone 4.

Cotoneasters will grow in any well-drained soil, even of poor quality. Full sun is best, but they can be expected to make good growth in part shade. Since plants of any size seldom can be moved successfully, they are offered by nurserymen in containers. These are easily transplanted. The usual method of increase is by cuttings.

Cotoneasters show their twiggy tracery to good advantage against rocks.

Cowberry—1'—Zone 5   *Vaccinium Vitis-Idaea*

An acid-soil plant of pleasing appearance when well grown in the right location, this dwarf evergreen cousin of the blueberry has small glossy leaves, pink bell-shaped flowers, and small red berries. Plants spread by underground stems, making a mass of even height, dense and pleasing in full sun, somewhat looser in appearance in the shade. There are two kinds, similar except in the size of the leaves and fruits. The mountain cranberry is the hardier of the two (*V. Vitis-Idaea minus*). Lowbush blueberry (*V. angustifolium laevifolium*) makes a most attractive ground cover in rocky, acid soil or where a naturalistic effect is desired. It has the added value of autumn color and its twiggy growth is of interest in winter.

Moist, acid soil in sun or shade meets the requirements of this plant. It is increased by root division and is often planted as sods sold by collectors or specialists in native plants.

Creeping Baby's-Breath—6"—Zone 3   *Gypsophila repens*

A favorite rock plant, with mats of silvery-gray foliage that trail on the ground, creeping baby's-breath makes a cover of crisp texture. This sturdy little perennial is suited to sunny situations. Delicate sprays of pink or white bloom make it most attractive for a period of 6 weeks or more in early summer. For drifts in rocky places, along walks and steps, or as a highly ornamental paving plant, it has real merit.

Well-drained soil, with plenty of lime added where soils are known to be acid, satisfies this alpine. Increase of plants can be accomplished by dividing the roots, by cuttings, or from seed.

Creeping Mint—2"—Zone 5   *Mentha requieni*

For sunny or shady walks and terraces, in the crevices of paved surfaces, creeping mint makes a mossy effect clouded with light purple flowers in early summer. The great charm of this microscopic jewel from Corsica lies in the pungent fragrance of the foliage, which fills the air when you tread this green carpet. It makes a delightful mat under taller plants.

It likes moist soil and spreads most willingly, but winter often takes its toll, though not permanently. It seeds freely and there are always odd bits in crevices that survive. Once you have it, it usually remains. Dealers in rock plants and herbs sell it.

Creeping Snowberry—2–3"—Zone 2   *Gaultheria hispidula*

Wild-flower enthusiasts have taught gardeners throughout the country to have keener powers of observation in the use of native plants. Creeping snowberry, or creeping pearlberry, is a native plant found in moist acid soil of peaty texture. It is one of those slow-growing evergreen carpets with oval leathery leaves, bell-shaped white flowers, and shiny china-white fruits in autumn. Both the foliage and the fruit have the flavor of wintergreen. A plant for sun or light shade, it can be established wherever its soil requirements can be met. Here is a delightful ground cover for the wild garden or among low-growing, acid-soil shrubs.

Handle it in mats or clumps, removing as much of the native soil as possible when transplanting it. Prepare soil with ample amounts of peat and leafmold. Water thoroughly until it is established.

Crested Iris—8"—Zone 2   *Iris cristata*

For the most part, irises hardly fit the category of ground covers, but the crested iris (*I. cristata*) makes a dense mat as its creeping rhizomes cover the soil on the surface. The crowded fans of sword-like foliage

Crested iris is noted for its showy blooms and attractive foliage.

are a welcome contrast to the small leaves of many ground covers. It grows in sun or shade and endures considerable acidity. Mass-planted along steps, on steep grades, among the seams of large rocks, or nestled at the base of a ledge, crested iris makes a dramatic accent. The flat blue or white flowers in May and June are profuse. Other low-growing species such as *I. pumila* and roof iris (*I. tectorum*) are useful for covering soil in full sun and sweet soil.

Crested iris is of easy culture in average garden soil. Increase it by division of the rhizomes after flowering. Set them on the surface of the soil and cover the roots only.

Daylily—1–3′—Zone 2   *Hemerocallis hybrids*

These big-scale perennials with their graceful foliage and showy blooms, available in literally hundreds of varieties, hardly strike us as ground covers. But when we consider their hardiness and their large root systems, their use as soil binders comes to mind. On slopes along railroad tracks and highways they have been used successfully. Along steep cuts on rural roads, they have special value. They take shade or sun with ease, are not particular as to soil, and withstand drought and the pests that trouble most plants. If the typical garden varieties

Naturalized daylilies make an ideal ground cover for country gardens.

appear too tall for a given situation, consider some of the dwarf kinds offered by growers.

Increase is by root division at almost any time during the growing season. Feeding with a complete fertilizer will get them off to a good start.

Dead Nettle—10"—Zone 4 *Lamium maculatum*

Although it tends to become weedy, spotted dead nettle is most attractive because of the conspicuous white markings on the dark green sturdy foliage. Purplish flowers appear in whorls from late spring to early summer. It develops large, sprawling clumps highlighting shady areas as it stands out in contrast to the somber green so prevalent everywhere. In late autumn the foliage takes on pink and purple tones which make the white spots all the more appealing, and it keeps its fresh appearance until temperatures become severe.

Ordinary soil in full sun or part shade suits it. Increase your stock by root division in spring or early fall.

Dichondra—2"—Zone 7 *Dichondra carolinensis*

Dichondra, a small-leaved matting perennial native to the southeastern states, has received considerable attention in recent years as a lawn substitute in the South and on the West Coast. Sometimes called lawn leaf or pony foot, it spreads by underground runners. The small kidney-shaped leaves, about a half inch across, have a tendency to grow somewhat larger, with longer stems, in shade. In its massed effect, it has the appearance of clover, and the resulting thick sod is usually $1\frac{1}{2}$ to 2 inches high. It is surprisingly tolerant as far as various types of soil are concerned, and has proved to be successful in both sun and shade. But, like most carpeting plants, it can be invaded by weeds, especially in its starting stages, and it tends to bunch so that it needs mowing when this condition occurs.

It has long been proved that any substitute for grass as far as lawn effects are concerned is at best a substitute, with special maintenance problems according to the climatic conditions under which it is grown. In areas of limited size where a flat mat is desired and lawn maintenance is not easy, dichondra has value. While it is widely claimed that dichondra kills out various types of lawn grass, it does not conquer Bermuda grass—at least in the California region—but rather covers it, giving a greener appearance in spring. This plant stands foot traffic, but suffers frost damage at 20°. However, it is a vigorous grower and self-sows readily.

To grow it, the soil is prepared as for a lawn and handled in the same manner. It is important that the seed be properly dried and bleached to assure good germination. It can also be planted from sods started in flats or from cuttings.

Dwarf Anchusa—1′—Zone 1   *Brunnera macrophylla*
                                               (*Anchusa myosotidiflora*)

Airy sprays of brilliant blue forget-me-not-like flowers on sturdy 15-inch stems in April and May are the prime features of this perennial ground cover. A tough, hardy, long-lived plant, with large, coarse, heart-shaped leaves, it self-sows readily. Since it blooms at daffodil time, it makes an ideal plant to combine with them in naturalized groups, among shrubs or large-scale perennial plantings, or in wild gardens. For a mixed ground-cover combination, use it with bleeding heart, the wood scillas, white violets, and other spring-flowering perennials for shady locations or in full sun. Although it thrives in full sun, it is equally well adapted to shade. In many catalogs, it is still listed as *Anchusa myosotidiflora* and called hardy forget-me-not.

Easy to grow and handle in ordinary garden soil, it tolerates considerable acidity. Space plants 18 inches apart. Increase is by division or seed. It self-sows readily and seedlings or root divisions can be set out at any time during the growing season.

DWARF ROSEMARY

Dwarf Rosemary—10″—Zone 7   *Rosmarinus officinalis prostratus*

California gardeners enjoy growing many desirable ground covers which are not hardy on the East Coast, particularly in New England. One of these, truly an outstanding dwarf shrub for sunny places, is the dwarf rosemary. It is a low-spreading form of the much treasured fragrant but tender shrub which is known as the herb sacred to remembrance. As the old garden writers used to say, it "quickens the memory and refreshes the spirit" every time a leaf is crushed. The carpeting form of rosemary seen in West Coast gardens makes a billowy mass for bank planting in the bright sun. Its dark green, narrow, evergreen leaves give it a refined appearance, and, when combined with gray foliage, it is all the more striking. Light blue flowers appear along the tips of the stems in early spring. The ideal places to use rosemary are along paths and steps, where it can be enjoyed at close range and crushed at will.

Full sun and well-drained gravelly soil suit it best. Little or no fertilizer is needed. It can take drought, for it is native to the Mediterranean countries. Stock can be increased by cuttings.

English Ivy—4–10″—Zone 5 *Hedera Helix*

Steeped in tradition, folklore, and history, English ivy is truly a beloved plant, rich in sentiment. Enduring in its beauty indoors and out, it is suited for climbing on walls, fences, and other kinds of support as much as it is utilized as a green carpet or ground cover. It is long-lived and persistent, even under trying conditions, but it is at its best in shady locations.

English ivy provides an effective setting for a garden bench.

English ivy ranks with pachysandra and myrtle as one of the most versatile ground covers in gardens here and abroad. The typical English form, so common everywhere, with its long, trailing stems, is ideal for northern or western exposures on banks, slopes, or level ground where other plants are not easy to establish and an evergreen cover is desired. Of a lustrous dark green, it has a richness and permanent quality possessed by few creeping plants. Various small-leaved varieties, some hardier than others, are used for underplanting beneath shrubs and to cover bare areas on terraces and irregular plots, in pergolas, or in difficult locations where green cover is needed. It gives a finished effect to shrub and perennial plantings. Ivies make an ideal setting for daffodils and the various kinds of little bulbs which flower in the spring, summer, and fall.

The conspicuous white veinings of the leaves of the green kinds, the wide variety in leaf pattern which makes the numerous horticultural forms appealing, and the bronzy autumn coloring of others are additional features of interest. A planting of ivy supplies ample foliage for indoor decoration at various seasons of the year.

Ivy has been widely hybridized so that there are many selected forms grown in various parts of the country, some hardier than others. The ideal sought in ivy is a type that can endure wind and winter sun without burning and can be grown in practically any type of soil. To most people, ivy is ivy, so long as it has the typical leaf and grows, but there are major differences. Baltic ivy (*H. Helix baltica*) has generally proved to be fairly hardy under difficult conditions and is widely planted, but it does not always prove itself.

A recent selection known as 238 St. English Ivy, developed by T. H. Everett of the New York Botanical Garden, is notable for its ability to withstand adverse conditions. It makes new growth earlier in the season than the type, keeps its color throughout the winter, and has proved to be extremely hardy under city winter conditions. Even in sunny locations, windswept areas, and cemeteries, it has shown its winter endurance. Trailing shoots are vigorous and stiff and spread laterally to make a pleasing pattern. Mature plants produce greenish flowers in rounded heads in autumn, followed by darkish fruits which persist through the winter.

The following list includes many of the varieties offered by growers. Some have been widely tested for hardiness and have proved themselves for selected areas. Others are known to be tender, but the best way to determine the most usable kinds for gardens where winters are severe is by testing. Location of an ivy planting as to winter sun and

(*Above*) English ivy links the various units of this planting.

(*Below*) Year-round beauty on a slope with English ivy.

general exposure usually reveals that some tender kinds can be grown in sheltered parts of the grounds even though they are not accepted as being partially or reliably hardy. This kind of pursuit is half the fun of gardening.

Arrowleaf (*saggitifolia*): Dull foliage, small in size, distinctive in form.

Baltic (*baltica*): A refined form of the type with smaller glossy leaves, generally claimed to be one of the hardiest of all.

Bulgaria: A hardy sport from the St. Louis area (see **Rumania,** below).

Bunchleaf (*conglomerata*): Slow-growing and stiff-branched with crimped leaves closely set, it is hardy to zero. Useful in sheltered locations for its texture and tailored effect.

(*Cavendishi*): Creamy-white margins give it distinction.

Crimean (*taurica*): Bright green in color with leaves much narrower than the species.

Finger-Leaf (*digitata*): Large, wide, dark green leaves with 5 to 7 lobes.

Foot-Leaf (*pedata*): Long, narrow middle lobes with white veining which accentuates the dark color of the foliage.

Glacier: A selected form hardy north to New Jersey.

Gold-Leaf (*aureo-variegata*): Yellow margins make it striking.

Hagenburger's Variegated: Long-leaved variegated form which has proved to be hardy as far north as New Jersey and is widely planted on the West Coast.

Heart-Leaved (*Helix cordata*): The almost black-green foliage assumes bronzy-purple coloring in the fall.

Irish (*hibernica*): Lighter green than the typical English ivy and usually larger, with short lobes, it is not so hardy as the species.

Marbled (*marmorata*): Similar to Irish ivy with yellowish-white markings.

Pittsburgh: Branches free from the leaf axils, making a very handsome appearance. Excellent for use in formal beds or tailored treatment of any kind.

Poets' (*poetica*): Wavy bright yellow-green foliage.

Rumania: This sport, and one named Bulgaria, introduced by Dr. Edgar Anderson of the Missouri Botanic Garden of St. Louis, serve the garden needs of this area for hardy English ivy.

Silver-Leaf (*argenteo-variegata*): Silvery-white variegated form, sometimes margined.

Stardust (*H. helix baltica* var.): A silvery variegated form of Baltic ivy.

Stripe-Leaf (*marginata*): A tender form with somewhat triangular leaf shape, irregular yellowish-white edge, and reddish striping in autumn.

Thorndale: This selection of English ivy developed in the Chicago area has proved to be satisfactory without protection for several decades.

Tree (*arborescens*): This form results when climbing forms reach the top of a support. The leaves are distinctly different from the rest of the plant, being almost without lobes. Green flowers appear, followed by dark fruits. When this growth is propagated, the resulting plants do not climb, but make small bushes instead.

Tricolor (*elegantissima*): Similar to Stripe-Leaf but with reddish edges.

Twisted (*tortuosa*): Leaves almost entirely in shape of curly form.

Other species of ivy include:

H. colchica: This rapid-growing form with light green foliage 5 to 10 inches long is only slightly lobed and heart-shaped. It is used from North Carolina south and along the West Coast. The variety *H. colchica dentata* has proved to be hardy near New York City in protected areas.

Algerian Ivy (*H. canariensis*): Large leaves 5 to 7 inches across, variable in outline and widely spaced on the stems. The variety Yellow-Edge has yellowish-white markings. Effective in tropical plantings and as a striking ground cover, it is hardy to Virginia and is widely used throughout the South and the Southwest.

H. nepalensis: This native of the Himalaya Mountains is a narrowly triangular-leaved kind to 4 inches long, tender in the Northeast, being hardy from Virginia south.

Ivy is easy to root from cuttings, or trailing stems with roots can be used. Some gardeners prefer to use hairpins or other means to peg down long trailers so that they will form roots. Wherever roots develop, pieces can be cut from the main plant and started anew. This is one of the great joys of growing ivy and one of the reasons for its widespread popularity and also for the fact that it can increase its ground-covering capacity with great rapidity.

Evergreen Candytuft—12″—Zone 4   *Iberis sempervirens*

Common perennial candytuft (*I. sempervirens*), which we grow in hardy borders and rock gordens, is actually a dwarf evergreen shrub of sprawling habit. Its crisp white flower clusters, which appear at tulip time and last for several weeks, are not the least of its merits. Evergreen foliage, clean growth, and longevity are points in its favor. On level areas or slopes in full sun or light shade, it holds its own throughout the year. By staggering the plants in a broad mass planting of candytuft, space is available for groups of tulips followed by such summer-flowering bulbs as montbretias, baby gladiolus, acidanthera, and others for summer color.

Several selected varieties are listed and these have merit, but they are not so rapid in their growth as *I. sempervirens* and thus not so well suited to cover large areas quickly. However, where a tailored, neat-growing cover is needed in formal plantings, these varieties are most useful. *Christmas Snow* blooms twice—first in May and June and again from early fall to hard frost. *Little Gem* is more dwarf than the type, only 6 inches tall and completely hardy. Leaves are smaller, delicate in texture. *Purity* is of comparable habit with unusually large flower

Evergreen candytuft provides a welcome note of white in spring.

heads. The species *I. gibraltarica* produces lilac or purple flowers, some-what earlier in the season. Because of its prolific blooming habit, it is not so permanent a plant as *I. sempervirens. Snowflake* has large flowers and foliage of greater substance than the type.

Well-drained soil of average fertility suits this plant. Start with small plants, bare root for early spring planting or pot-grown for later use. Stock can be increased by division of clumps or by cuttings rooted in sand and peat moss or from seed. Remember that large clumps have sizable root systems and do not transplant easily. An annual feeding with a complete fertilizer and heavy shearing after bloom will benefit the plants greatly.

Fig-Marigold—Zone 5–7   *Mesembryanthemum species*

West Coast gardeners refer to these desert plants as fig-marigolds or ice-plants. They include both annual and perennial kinds, are easily recognized by their fleshy stems, their trailing habit of growth, and their brilliantly colored flowers. The foliage is covered with watery, glistening bubbles resembling crystals of ice. They thrive by the sea and are used for holding shifting sand banks, steep banks, slopes, and highway cuts. Although some are rather coarse, they are most colorful and flourish without water in hot, dry places. Masses of these flowers in bloom are real eye-catchers. Only a few kinds are known and grown in the East, but they have possibilities for wider use as temporary ground covers in cold climates. Botanists have reclassified these South African natives under different names, but they are commonly referred to as mesembryanthemums.

Ordinary soil on the poor side suits them. Give these tropical plants full sun. They can endure drought and wind. The annual kinds are raised from seed and self-sow readily. Perennial types are propagated by cuttings. These plants, although rugged as to soil and exposure, are extremely sensitive to frost.

Fleeceflower—1′—Zone 5   *Polygonum Reynoutria*

Fleeceflower is a pretty name and the color illustrations of a plant known as *Polygonum Reynoutria* that appear in catalogs are most at-tractive. The common name is not well known to most gardeners, but, to many, polygonum means Mexican bamboo, one of the worst pests known to gardeners. The Reynoutria fleeceflower (*P. Reynoutria*), also called dwarf lace plant, averages 1 foot in height. This introduction from a leading English nursery has rather coarse foliage, but its red stems and creamy flowers are pleasing. A useful ground cover in sun or shade, it thrives where other plants, including most ground covers, are not satisfactory.

This perennial spreads by underground stems which root as they grow, and the smallest segment will produce a new plant. Sun or shade and ordinary soil are its requirements. Its invasive habits must be remembered when choosing a place to use it.

Foam Flower—1'—Zone 4   *Tiarella cordifolia*

One of the loveliest and daintiest native carpeting plants found in moist woodlands from Nova Scotia to Georgia and Alabama and westward to Michigan is appropriately named foam flower for its feathery spikes of bloom, which appear in early spring well above the foliage. This native perennial adapts itself easily to cultivation. Other common names are false mitre-wort, for its similarity to *Mitella diphylla,* and

Foam flower and other wildings in a shady corner.

coolwort. Maple-like leaves of darkish green sometimes marked with brown make an even, soft-textured mass throughout the growing season. Here is a shade-loving plant for moist places or average garden soil. It can be used as mixed cover with other native plants or in drifts by itself.

Root division in spring or fall is the way to increase your stock. It requires little attention and spreads moderately to carpet a given area.

Forget-Me-Not—6–10″—Zone 5   *Myosotis scorpioides*

Forget-me-nots have a way of establishing themselves once planted to make a charming natural ground cover in shady places, or even in the sun. In this respect, few of our spring flowers are more colorful and more adaptable. The forms usually planted are not true perennials, but annual or biennial in habit. The true perennial form (*M. scorpioides*) is the most desirable, since it blooms over a long period. The variety *semperflorens* is especially preferable because of its permanence. The ideal way to use forget-me-nots in gardens is to have them in abundance as filler plants for their delicate, airy effect, and for color among plants of bolder foliage, where they are all the more appealing. In bog gardens, or along streams or brooks, they are truly at home. Somehow, when regimented in straight rows, they seem out of place.

Plants can be increased by division or from seed, or self-sown seedlings. Moist soil and some shade are needed to establish forget-me-nots.

Fringed Bleeding-Heart—15″—Zone 2   *Dicentra eximia*

Many city and suburban gardens have dull, shady corners that could be made more attractive with ground covers. Among the best perennials for such use is the fringed or plumy bleeding-heart. Of attractive habit, with ferny, blue-green foliage and showy, rosey-pink, heart-shaped flowers, it blooms from early spring until well into the summer, requiring little or no care. It forms sizable clumps 2 feet or more in diameter, spreading from the crown, and self-sows readily. Often the seedlings take root close to a foundation or garden wall and quickly develop into attractive free-blooming plants. Both blooms and foliage are desirable for cuttings.

Fringed bleeding-heart combines well with ferns, wild flowers, and spring-flowering bulbs. It has a place under flowering shrubs, between various kinds of broad-leaved evergreens, and in shady perennial borders. The hybrid *Bountiful* is a very superior plant with larger flowers of deeper color that does well in full sun or in shade. *Debutante*, with blush-pink flowers; *Paramount*, a lively red; and *Silversmith*, an

Plumy bleeding heart is noted for its delicately cut foliage and free-blooming habit.

ivory-white, are among the most recent additions to the list. These varieties are notable for their adaptability to sun or shade and their prolonged flowering habit. The bleeding-heart of old-time gardens, *D. spectabilis,* makes a taller ground cover for spring gardens and self-sows readily in shade, but its foliage disappears in midsummer. For wild gardens there is Dutchman's-breeches (*D. Cucullaria*), with white flowers tipped with yellow on 6-inch stems.

Sun or shade and average well-drained garden soil suit the bleeding-hearts. Plants tend to grow somewhat taller in the shade. Divide clumps in early spring or late summer, or look for seedlings near the parent plant or, indeed, almost anywhere in the garden.

Galax—6″—Zone 2   *Galax aphylla*

Gardeners who enjoy choice plants are always enthusiastic about such uncommon kinds as galax, an outstanding, broad-leaved, ever-green perennial. Common names are galaxy and beetleweed. At the turn of the century, florists began to use quantities of galax leaves in all types of floral designs. The demand for these green and reddish-bronze leaves, cut from the forest floor of our southeastern woodlands, was of some importance commercially for many years. Yet, the plants have persisted in the wild. Even without flowers, the leathery texture and the glossy sheen of the leaves are enough to recommend it. The stately flower spikes which appear in late June or July, rising a foot or more above the foliage, gleam like white tapers in shady nooks.

Consider this gem as a companion for other acid-loving kinds from the Carolina mountains, such as shortia, pieris, leucothoe, azaleas, and rhododendrons, or as an underplanting among any group of broad-leaved plants. Here is a plant to challenge the home gardener who has a woodland setting and is eager to have unusual ground covers, since galax is not always easy to establish.

Galax requires a moist, peaty soil, rich in leafmold, and a shady location, and needs to have its place deeply prepared in the garden. Early spring is the best time to plant it in northern gardens, but where the autumn season is long and winters are not normally severe, it can be set out in the early fall. Large clumps can be divided to increase your stock. Nurseries specializing in native plants are the usual source of supply.

Galax, an aristocrat among ground covers for acid-soil plantings.

Germander—1′—Zone 4   *Teucrium Chamaedrys*

Used for generations in gardens as a low hedge, this dwarf evergreen shrub has many good points as a ground cover. Its small, glossy, evergreen foliage and billowy appearance are refreshing at all seasons of the year, especially so in late autumn and winter. During hard winters it often burns badly but sprouts in the spring from its heavy root system. In summer it sports rosy-purple flowers in whorls at the tops of the stems. A dwarf form (*T. Chamaedrys prostratum*) is several inches lower and even better suited as a glossy carpet plant. For formal effects where green blocky masses are needed or for informal cover purposes, germander fills the bill.

Well-drained soil on the gritty side suits it best, with full sun or light shade. It is easy to propagate by division or from cuttings taken in June. Creeping stems make it a slowly matting plant. Shearing annually thickens growth and greatly improves the plant. If done in June, a ready-made supply of cuttings is at hand. Set plants 1 foot apart.

Gill-over-the-Ground—6″—Zone 2   *Glecoma hederacea*

This is a plant with enough poetic names of folk origin to make one think of it as something to be cherished. But, to most gardeners, it belongs in that category of plants that do not belong in the garden. It's a weed. The foliage is clean and attractive; so too are the purplish flowers. It spreads by underground runners with amazing rapidity, especially in moist, shady places, but grows with ease in sun also. There is a variegated form with white and pink markings which is most attractive and less invasive.

This plant often appears in lists of ground covers and is included here to warn the unwary gardener. It is by no means as difficult to eradicate as many of our naturalized and native weeds, but this fact does not change its status.

Gold-Dust—1′—Zone 4   *Alyssum saxatile*

Practically every rock garden in America has some form of hardy perennial alyssum. The gray-toned foliage and showy heads of bloom, plus its ability to make a large sprawling mass, are advantages for covering soil. A plant suited to rocky areas where cover is a problem, it is at its best in full sun and gritty soil. The common kind with brilliant yellow flowers in April and May is known as *Gold-Dust, Basket-of-Gold,* and *Golden Tuft.* There is a double-flowered variety, a popular pale-yellow kind (*A. saxatile citrinum*), and a recent introduction called

Gold Dust and snow-in-summer provide an abundance of color on this slope.

Dudley Neville which is much more dwarf than the type and has pleasing sulfur-yellow blooms. Another species, about 1 foot tall, with wiry, woody stems, listed as *A. argenteum,* has small silvery leaves and large flat heads of yellow bloom in summer.

Start with young plants from pots, or rooted cuttings, or all of these types can be raised from seed. Alyssum has a tap root and is almost impossible to move successfully, once it is established in a planting. Full sun, ordinary soil, and good drainage are all it needs. Clip off the flower heads after bloom has passed and shear the plants hard to promote compact growth and an abundance of new foliage which keeps its neat appearance all summer.

Goldthread—4″—Zone 2   *Coptis species*

In the cool damp woodlands of the Northeast, the tiny evergreen goldthread (*C. trifolia*) makes shiny carpets of leaves with tiny white blossoms. It spreads by underground runners which are as yellow as gold, hence the common name. A species from the arctic regions (*C. groenlandica*) is even more dwarf in habit. From Japan we have *C. quinquifolia,* with 5-lobed leaves instead of the customary 3 found on the two kinds above. The waxy white flowers appear early in spring. These are plants for dense shade in moist acid soil for carpeting under various kinds of evergreens. Oftentimes there is need for a flat carpet to give finish to naturalistic planting bordering a shady terrace or walk. Where an unusual type of cover is desired, one of these tiny plants may be the plant to fill the need.

Clumps or sods can be divided to increase the supply. Moist acid soil and shade, even fairly dense, suit this plant.

Goutweed—8″—Zone 3   *Aegopodium Podograria variegatum*

Both the botanical and the common names of this hardy perennial will discourage many gardeners from planting this plant. To some who have had experience with it, it is among the worst of weeds and a "cussed" nuisance. Yet, others find it desirable for carpeting areas under such trees as maples where cover of any kind is difficult to maintain, or for planting on banks and other bare areas. The plain green form of goutweed is not much planted. However, the variegated form, with its attractive green-and-white leaves produced on creeping rootstocks, makes a most effective mottled carpet, especially in shade. Flat white carrot-like flowers appear in June. Goutweed grows anywhere it can take root, in sun or shade. Despite its bad reputation, it can be kept within bounds by most gardeners who choose to use it.

The smallest bit of its creeping root will start a new plant, and it can be moved at any time during the growing season. Usually, where

Goutweed replaces grass under a maple.

it is used for ground cover, it can be kept under control more easily in poor soil. The first hard frost kills the foliage.

Hall's Honeysuckle—18–24″—Zone 5   *Lonicera japonica halliana*

The most widely used vine for covering banks and slopes in many parts of the country, it can also be the meanest of pests to eradicate. It has clean foliage and delightfully fragrant flowers and will grow anywhere in any kind of soil. On the other hand, it makes a tangled mat of growth and twines itself around shrubs and trees. In many areas it is disliked because birds drop seeds of poison ivy, which thrive in its dense growth. When neglected, it can become a breeding place for various kinds of weed trees and, because it is so resistant to the elements and is often allowed to grow without pruning or restraining, it has rightfully earned the name of pest. Unless carefully restrained, Hall's honeysuckle is not suited to the small home grounds or to any restricted area. When it is cut back annually and kept in check, it is most attractive. Where there is ample room for it to spread, its value lies in its ability to make quick cover and bind soils on slopes and banks. It is also a very inexpensive plant to use.

Any type of soil suits it, in sun or shade. It is increased by division of the roots.

Harebell—9″—Zone 3   *Campanula species*

The harebell, or tussock bell flower, makes a handsome carpet to enjoy in the warm days of summer, although most gardeners do not use it that way. The foliage of this low perennial is attractive in itself, for it starts as a tight tuft and opens to a trim cushion a foot or more across, but not more than 6 inches high. The cup-shaped flowers rise well above the foliage to make a bountiful display, in June, continuing with a sprinkling of bloom until early fall. The type has clear blue flowers and there is a pure white variety. *Blue Carpet,* with deep blue flowers, is noted for prolific bloom. Several other species have merit as ground covers for limited use. Among these are *C. poscharskyana,* a trailing type with violet flowers on a 5-inch plant. The dainty bluebell of Scotland (*C. rotundifolia*) makes mats of foliage only a few inches tall and holds its swaying bells of the fairest blue imaginable on wiry stems 1 foot or more tall. It frequently self-sows, appearing in the most unexpected places. All these campanulas (and several not included) have merit as paving plants on terraces and in drifts along paths and walks.

Full sun or part shade and ordinary well-drained gritty soil suit these plants. Increase is by division in early spring or late summer, or they can also be raised from seed. In flat areas where water might stand in winter, the soil needs to have coarse gravel added to insure good drainage.

HEATH AND HEATHER

Heath—4–15"—Zone 5	*Erica species*
Irish Heath—18"—Zone 5	*Daboecia cantabrica*
Spike Heath—6"—Zone 5	*Bruckenthalia spiculifolia*
Heather—6–24"—Zone 4	*Calluna species*

These low-growing shrubs are a joy at almost any season of the year. They are steeped in sentiment and tradition, and part of their appeal rests in the mind's eye for those who have walked the moors in the British

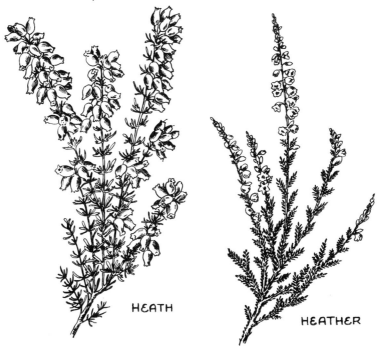

HEATH

HEATHER

Isles and picked their own nosegays of heather and gorse in the August sunshine. In the Northwest so many kinds are cultivated that gardeners enjoy bloom from some species or variety every month of the year. In the Northeast, heather (*Calluna*) has become naturalized, to some extent, in sandy soils, often near the coast.

Unlike many ground covers which are planted in shade, the heaths

and the heathers are for open spaces exposed to full sun and wind. Use them in large irregular groups, often with several kinds planted together, for continuity of bloom. Settings for houses on slopes can be greatly enhanced with a heather lawn, interspersed with weathered rocks. In fact, for hot, dry situations, this kind of cover, ranging in height from 4 inches to 1 foot or more, is decidedly picturesque and more suitable than grass. Companion plants for use with them include sand myrtle with its dark green foliage; thyme, with its flat matting effect; and blue fescue and thrift, with their grassy texture. Sheets of heather blending into the dark glossy green of bearberry make a dramatic contrast on a slope or on fairly level areas. These are excellent landscape materials for broad sweeping carpets. In small gardens, treat them as a unit of the planting rather than as specimens spotted here and there.

The heaths (species and varieties of *Erica*) have needle-like leaves, sometimes with a bluish cast, while others are yellow-green. These include winter-blooming kinds as well as spring- and summer-flowering types. Related kinds include the spike heath (*Bruckenthalia spiculifolia*) with pink flowers in early summer on plants 1 foot high, and Irish heath (*Daboecia cantabrica*), with dainty white, purple, or pink bell-like flowers borne in graceful spikes from summer to early fall.

These miniature matting shrubs are not difficult to grow if their soil requirements are met and the right site is chosen for them. Peaty, sandy soil on a slight slope is the kind of place they like and where they show to best advantage. It also assures good drainage, which is vital to their permanence. Naturally rocky areas or those where weathered rocks are introduced add to the naturalized effect of the setting chosen. Full sun or high shade that gives filtered sunlight in the heat of summer results in good bloom. They will grow in a fair amount of shade but bloom is usually sparse.

> *Erica carnea: Spring Heath.* Widely grown for its early spring bloom (February to May, according to locality). Plants are a foot high or less. Varieties include:
>
> *King George.* Rosy crimson blooms. This variety received an award of merit from the Royal Horticultural Society.
>
> *Ruby Glow.* Rich ruby color.
>
> *Springwood White.* Of dwarf trailing habit with white flowers and light green foliage, it rates high.
>
> *Springwood Pink.* An equally good pink-flowering form; like its white companion, this carpeting form is only 3 or 4 inches high.

Heather brightens the summer landscape with pink and white bloom.

Creeping junipers border a heather lawn in a Cape Cod garden.

Vivelli. Carmine-red bells with red-toned foliage in autumn.

E. ciliaris: Fringed or Dorset Heath. Tender in the colder regions of the Northeast, yet it usually sends up new growth from the ground. The grayish-pink bells appear in September, but there are several varieties which bloom a month earlier.

E. cinerea: Twisted Heath. These are summer-flowering kinds, considered quite drought-resistant when established.

    atrorubens. Dome-like in form, slender arching stems with deep-red bells in July and August.

    C. D. Eason. Bright rich red flowers, it is conspicuous in summer.

    Golden Drop. Yellowish foliage which changes to russet and red in winter. Pink flowers appear in summer.

    violacea. More upright than the variety mentioned above, bearing large spikes of bold purple.

E. darleyensis: Darley or Winter Heath. A vigorous grower, big-scale in its habit, to 2 feet or more, this mound-shaped plant bears pinkish-lilac bloom through the winter months in mild climates and early spring in the Northeast.

E. Tetralix: Bell-Flowered or Cross-Leaved Heath. Downy-gray foliage and flowers of waxy texture add to the charm of this species.

    alba mollis. White bells borne aloft on stiff, twiggy branches in profusion through the summer months.

    George Fraser. The pale-pink flowers and bluish foliage are most attractive.

E. vagans: Cornish Heath. Plants range from 1 to 2 feet in height, according to variety, with showy bloom in fluffy whorls in summer.

    alba minor. A dwarf white form.

    Lyonesse. A white-flowered variety of merit.

    Mrs. D. F. Maxwell. An upright grower with dark green foliage and long spikes of vivid pink bloom, it performs from early summer to autumn.

    St. Keverne. Clear pink flowers appear in clusters at the tips of the stems and it blooms for a long period in late summer.

In contrast, the heathers (species and varieties of *Calluna*) have scale-like overlapping leaves that give them the appearance of miniature junipers. There are distinct yellow-leaved kinds and bronzy-tipped forms, as well as the typical soft greens. Some take on bronzy or purplish tones as the temperature drops. Heather is known as ling in Scotland. To find a sprig of white heather is considered good luck and, if carried or worn, assures a safe return to the place whence it came. Flowers appear in loose sprays and may be white, pink, lavender or purple.

Calluna vulgaris. Plants vary in height from 4 inches to 2 feet or more, according to variety. The dwarf forms, those of medium height, and the tall growers—when grouped in broad masses on a slight slope or sandy knoll—are enchanting.

alba rigida. Dwarf and spreading in habit, with white flowers.

alporti. Tall, upright grower, deep crimson on a fuzzy-leaved plant.

aurea. Coppery foliage in dwarf mounds with pink flowers.

Camla. Of low, spreading habit, the flowers are double light pink.

County Wicklow. Bright pink flowers on a dwarf plant.

cuprea. Golden-yellow foliage which turns bronzy in autumn.

Foxii nana. One of the smallest of all, forming a tight cushion with tiny spikes of purple bells.

J. B. Hamilton. Less than 1 foot tall, of compact habit with arching stems of bright pink flowers beginning in early summer.

Hammondii. A tall grower, noted for its sturdy habit with white flowers.

Johnson's variety. Lavender bloom in late fall.

H. E. Beale. Double silvery-pink on long stems, it rates among the best and reaches 2 feet or more when in flower.

Kuphaldti. A dwarf plant of twisted growth only a few inches tall, and pinkish-lavender bloom.

Mrs. Ronald H. Gray. A true dwarf with carpets of lavender bloom and emerald-green foliage.

nana compacta. Dainty moss-like growth and lavender-pink bloom.

searlei. A late-flowering white of low habit.

Tib. A foot or more tall with red-purple bloom from early summer to late autumn.

Winter damage is a factor with the heaths. During severe winters it can be serious, causing the stems to split. When this occurs, plants must be cut back to encourage new growth from the base. Yet, the heathers suffer badly from winter wind and sunburn when snow cover is not sufficient. Open winters take their toll of even the sturdiest of plants and sometimes finish them. The practical way to handle this problem with heath and heather is to provide cover with evergreen boughs, something of a nuisance but well worth the effort. Heavy shearing of damaged specimens in *early* spring will encourage new growth and restore the plants to their former vigor.

Heather, thrift, and thyme used to make an interesting pattern.

A path of thyme bordered with heather and gray-foliaged herbs.

Early spring is the ideal time to set out the heaths and the heathers. Rooted cuttings from pots or field-grown clumps are offered by most specialists and nurserymen. If rooted cuttings from flats are used, protect the delicate roots from drying out. Whenever possible, prepare soil in the autumn and leave it in a rough state over winter. A mixture of equal parts of well-rotted cow manure or compost and peat moss (obtained from local bogs) added to the existing sandy soil supplies the organic matter needed by the roots. Soil preparation should be at least 1 foot deep. If done in the spring, allow a few weeks for the soil to settle before planting. Thorough watering is needed after planting and attention to this chore is essential for the first year. While these hardy shrubs can endure considerable drought, they may need a thorough soaking occasionally in extremely dry spells, unless your soil has abundant organic material.

Plants may be increased by dividing established clumps in spring, by layering, and by cuttings. Of these methods, layering is the easiest for most home gardeners. Heaths growing in large masses tend to layer naturally as the lower branches trail or come in contact with the soil. Layering can be induced by mounding soil over the lower stems and pinning them down or by placing a stone on a branch to hold it close to the soil. Another method is to heap soil up around the crown of the plant to induce stems to produce roots. These rooted portions can be cut from the mother plant and set out where they can be given care until they are large enough for permanent planting. Some gardeners keep them in a cold frame the first winter, as with rooted cuttings. It is a mistake to put young plants in permanent places in full sun unless they can be given frequent watering.

Cuttings of half-ripened wood made in late June usually root in 4 to 5 weeks in a covered frame or propagating case. Strip the foliage from the lower portion of the stem, being careful not to injure the thin bark. Insert in sandy peat and keep moist until roots are well formed. Then transplant to a cold frame for the first winter.

Houseleek—1–3″—Zone 4   *Sempervivum tectorum*

The common houseleek or sempervivum (*S. tectorum*), frequently referred to as hen-and-chickens, has been growing in American gardens for 300 years. This curious plant, with its rosettes of fleshy leaves, gathers its young around it in a cushion or mat. It fills the seams of rocks with ease and is sometimes used along rocky paths in the sun. On dry slopes as a ground cover, especially where soil is poor and gritty, it flourishes and crowds out most weeds. If interplanted with sedums,

Houseleeks on a rocky slope make an unusual patterned effect.

especially such weedy kinds as *Sedum acre,* it is soon crowded. Best left to itself, or planted with other varieties (of which there are quantities), it makes a flat, uneven cover of crisp texture and color, depending on the kinds used.

Houseleeks are ideal rock cover in sunny places, for they fit so compactly into the space at hand as to belong. For softening rough edges and making highlights in the rock surfaces, these succulent-leaved rosettes were made to order. Where soil pockets are of varying depths, other species of plants are also desirable, but in shallow nooks and crannies with scarcely any soil the houseleek is the easy solution. The stubby flower spikes in summer add greatly to their ornamental value.

Houseleeks can be planted at almost any time during the growing season. Drainage is much more vital to their survival than soil. No wet feet for them at any season. Use them first of all in sunny places, but they can endure light shade.

Ivy Geranium—12–18″—Zone 7   *Pelargonium peltatum*

Ivy-leaved geraniums are among the many colorful plants used to cover ground on slopes and low banks in California. The practice is frequently featured in parking strips and in gardens.

This trailing plant is valued for its attractive glossy, ivy-like foliage and large, showy clusters of brightly colored flowers in a wide variety of pink, white, rose, lilac, purple, salmon-pink, red, and deep red. Of rapid growth, the plants prefer a light, sandy loam with leafmold added. They grow in full sun or partial shade and tolerate wind—another point in their favor.

Plants need to be cut back annually in early spring to keep them from getting leggy. Fertilizing should be on the sparse side; watering should give needed moisture but never be excessive.

Jacob's Ladder—1′—Zone 3   *Polemonium reptans*

Of little value as an all-season cover plant, but delightful for a spring carpet, Jacob's ladder (*Polemonium reptans*) is one of those old-time hardy perennials which persists and spreads in shade. Set among ferns, it makes a show before the fronds are fully developed. In dry summers, the foliage becomes practically dormant. Plants grow up to 1 foot tall, depending on the soil fertility, and their loose heads of soft blue literally cover the fern-like foliage. Well suited to half-shade, it does equally well in sun.

Of easy culture, it can be divided at almost any season of the growing year, quickly developing sizable clumps by means of its thick creeping rootstocks. It self-sows frequently and ordinary garden soil suits it.

Junipers—1–2′—Zones 2–5   *Juniperus species*

On steep slopes in full sun where grass is difficult to maintain because soil tends to be dry and erosion threatens, few plants are more adaptable and desirable than low-growing junipers. Horizontal in habit, evergreen and soft in texture, these prostrate types are attractive throughout the year. As the branches spread they root, making a wavy carpet. Creeping junipers are often the answer to problems created by the construction of split-level houses, particularly in areas of rolling terrain. Also, when used in masses to link several changes of level on home grounds, they are more effective than grass because of their height, color, texture, and mode of growth.

For contrast in texture, combine low-growing junipers with pachysandra.

Low-growing junipers and other ground covers enhance the beauty of ledges.

Most widely planted is the creeping juniper (*J. horizontalis*), which makes a dense mat of gray-green needle-like foliage. For color and variety the blue-gray Waukegan juniper (*J. horizontalis douglasi*) makes a pleasing companion plant. For stronger blue-green color, you can use the blue creeping juniper (*J. horizontalis glauca*), a slower and more compact grower. Another variety in wide use is the Andorra juniper, valued for its delicate texture and rich purple color during autumn and winter.

The Sargent juniper (*J. chinensis sargenti*) is of more billowy habit and somewhat taller as it matures. It is grayish-green and somewhat bolder in habit than the common creeping types.

The Japanese garden juniper (*J. procumbens*) is darker in color, dense and rather upright in habit, and about 2 feet tall when mature.

The common juniper of rocky soils in upland pastures, listed as *J. communis depressa*, is a wide-spreading plant which may eventually grow 3 feet tall, but usually is lower. Gray-green and silvery in texture, it is especially desirable where there is space to accommodate it in naturalistic plantings. Bluish fruits add interest in autumn and winter. Of more compact habit, the mountain form (*J. communis saxatilis*) makes broad patches slightly under 2 feet in height.

For sandy banks and slopes, the shore juniper (*J. conferta*), a Japanese native, is a real asset, especially close to the sea, since it is not harmed by salt spray. Bright green shoots grow somewhat upright from low, spreading branches. Plants are 1 foot or less in height and spread 8 to 10 feet across, hugging the ground.

Regardless of how poor the soil is or appears to be, junipers will prosper with proper soil preparations. Assuming that the slope has been raked and graded, dig holes wide and deep enough to accommodate equal parts of garden soil and peat moss thoroughly mixed with a handful of acid-soil fertilizer. Water thoroughly and leave a slight depression around each plant to catch water. Additional water will be needed twice a week until the plants are established. Rooted cuttings from flats, potted plants, or balled and burlapped specimens may be used.

Year-round beauty is achieved with low-growing junipers, periwinkle, and dwarf yews.

Kenilworth Ivy—4–6″—Zone 5   *Cymbalaria muralis*

Kenilworth ivy is a weedy trailer for rock gardens, along steps and walls, or to soften the edges of a terrace in the shady parts of the garden. Its miniature light green leaves, shaped somewhat like those of the grape, and its tiny mauve flowers similar to snapdragons are appealing because of their size. A ground cover of limited use, it is hardier than it looks but needs a sheltered location. Even when patches die out, it reappears from seedlings or bits that have found their way into some protected cranny.

Reginald Farrer, the great English plant explorer and rock-garden expert, has described *C. aequitriloba* as "A Tiny Tim of extraordinary charm." Not a plant for wide use in the Northeast, where it is tender, it is another of those little jewels for shady walks and terraces where its lacy tracery can be enjoyed as it trails over rocky surfaces.

Moist rich loam and a shady location are needed to keep this plant happy. It spreads by rapidly trailing stems which root as they run, and is easily divided.

Lady's-mantle has appealing foliage and soft yellow bloom.

Lady's-Mantle—15"—Zone 4   *Alchemilla vulgaris*

An old-time perennial not widely cultivated in present-day gardens, lady's-mantle is valued primarily for its grayish-green leaves which are distinctly lobed and hold drops of dew, making a delightful effect on a summer morning. The yellowish flowers are not particularly exciting, but the foliage makes a good ground cover in full sun or light shade, and provides a pleasing texture. It spreads by creeping rootstocks.

Ordinary garden soil suits it and it flourishes in full sun or part shade. Stock is easily increased by root division.

Lamb's-Ears—1'—Zone 5   *Stachys lanata*

This low perennial named lamb's-ears, or lamb's-tongue, vividly describes the appearance of the gray woolly foliage. It is also called woolly betony. In rock gardens and herb plantings where its texture is valued, and as an edging plant, it has been commonly grown for centuries. As a ground cover for limited areas in sunny, well-drained, slightly sloping areas, it is a plant to remember, giving the effect of coolness in hot weather. Thinking of heather plantings interspersed with patches of thrift, here is another companion plant for sandy mounds. Great sheets of lamb's-ears used in front of pink floribunda roses in a seaside garden created a picture I shall long remember. In another effective way, this gray-textured perennial has been used as a foreground for coral bells. Spikes of reddish-purple bloom, 1 foot or more tall, appear in early summer, but some gardeners cut them off, preferring the silvery mats of foliage for their enduring beauty throughout the entire growing season.

Full sun and ordinary light soil, even of gritty texture, suit it best. When grown in heavy loam or in a fair amount of shade, it languishes and rots and looks sick. Division of clumps, which are of creeping habit, can be done at any time during the growing season.

Lantana—12–18"—Zone 7   *Lantana montevidensis*

Trailing or weeping lantana, favorite flower for hanging baskets, window boxes, and terrace planters, rates high as a ground cover in Florida, the Gulf states, and the southwestern desert area, and on the West Coast. Its northern limit for hardiness is central Texas and South Carolina. When it loses its leaves in cold spells and dies to the ground in frost, it can be expected to sprout again in the spring. However, in the Northeast it is essentially a tender plant, treated as an annual, but can be used most effectively as a temporary cover. Because of its woody stems and trailing habit, it makes a sturdy cover plant for large areas in full sun on level areas or slopes. Pinkish-lavender blooms, borne in clusters and carried at the ends of the trailing stems, are typical of the species. The yellow and white hybrids are especially effective.

A well-drained, light sandy loam suits it best. It flowers heavily in full sun, endures drought, and tolerates considerable wind, a strong point in its favor. Little or no feeding, sparse watering, and heavy pruning in early spring to keep plants from becoming woody are the easy requirements for growing lantana. Stock is increased by cuttings.

Lavender Cotton—15″—Zone 5   *Santolina Chamaecyparissus*

This dwarf spreading shrub often seen in herb gardens, sometimes as a dwarf hedge, can be used most effectively as a ground cover in sunny places, among rocks, or in any gritty soil. Of loose, open habit, its great charm lies in the pungent, silvery-gray evergreen foliage which gives it a distinctive appearance and texture. Its effect is heightened when planted with masses of bright green foliage of coarser texture. The yellow button-like flowers, which appear in summer, are of little consequence.

Lavender cotton has the same kind of appeal as the various silvery-leaved wormwoods, but is usually not as long-lived in most gardens. Spilling over ledges, easy slopes, or low walls, it blends well with thyme, winter savory, and germander to create a drift of old-time fragrance. For

Lavender cotton adds a welcome note of gray.

a trim, formal ground cover it can be sheared. A plant of year-round appeal, its pleasing winter aspect is a point to remember.

A kind with dark green leaves (*S. virens*), otherwise similar in habit, is most attractive. *S. virens ericoides* is a selected form of emerald-green. *S. neapolitana,* from southern Italy, is an unusual and little-known species, formerly listed as *S. rosmarinifolia*. It grows 2 feet tall or more in mild climates. The thread-like, pendulous foliage is silvery and shaggy. It is tender and needs protection where winter temperatures go below zero. Cutting it to the ground annually is recommended.

Plants can be set out at any time during the growing season. A well-drained location in full sun and poor soil suits this Mediterranean plant. Rooted cuttings from pots or flats are the most satisfactory way to handle it in quantity. Most nurseries offer 2-year plants, either field-grown or from containers. Old clumps benefit from heavy pruning in early spring, a practice often necessary after an open winter.

Lily-of-the-Valley—6"—Zone 2   *Convallaria majalis*

In many gardens where lilies-of-the-valley were first planted in neat clumps, they have spread to become ground covers in sun and shade. Although not evergreen in foliage, they produce a dense mat of underground roots to hold soil. Soft green leaves, fragrant white bell-shaped flowers in May, and golden autumn foliage coloring are assets, but the foliage becomes unsightly as it fades. This point, and the fact that the ground remains bare all winter, are to be considered when choosing a place for lilies-of-the-valley. Yet, where there are large bare areas of soil to be covered, this tough, hardy perennial is effective, inexpensive, and desirable. A good ground cover under shrubs, it combines well with ferns. *Fortin's Giant* is an improved form with larger flower spikes than the type, and there is also a pale-pink variety.

Clumps can be divided at any time during the growing season, separating each rooted segment, or pip, as they are called. For a thick planting, set the pips 6 to 8 inches apart. Ordinary soil meets their requirements. Regular feeding with a complete fertilizer improves the size and quality of both foliage and flowers.

Lily-Turf—8–18"—Zone 5   *Liriope spicata*
Ophiopogon japonicus

Lily-turf is the common name of two related evergreen perennials, liriope and ophiopogon, which are the best known and most widely used ground covers in the lower South, particularly in Florida. Both are completely hardy and are easily adaptable to various types of soil.

(*Above*) Lily turf makes a richly textured mass effect.

(*Below*) Lilies-of-the-valley are well suited to shady places.

They endure heat, drought, and salt spray. Carpets of lily-turf are used in all degrees of shade, under trees and shrubs, on slopes and banks, as wide edging plants, and wherever soil cover is required. Plants make solid mats of growth quickly, which adds greatly to their value for erosion and dust control. Both are native to the Orient.

The flower spikes of liriope, which resemble those of grape hyacinth, may be blue or white. These are held well above the foliage, whereas the blooms of ophiopogon are mostly concealed in the leaves. Fruits are blue-black berries which appear in the fall. Of the two, liriope is taller.

There are several distinct types of ophiopogon. *O. japonicus* is a dwarf form usually less than 1 foot tall and grows less rapidly than liriope. In this respect it has merit for use in small areas. *O. Jaburan* is taller in habit. Both liriope and ophiopogon have forms with yellow-striped foliage which has definite ornamental value when used for accent.

Ophiopogon has proved itself hardy in Washington, D. C., and can be grown even farther north in protected locations. Liriope is hardier and can be depended on to live over winter in the Boston area. However, in winter, its color in no way compares with such cover plants as myrtle, pachysandra, pachistima, and others. Both of these popular Florida ground covers have been widely advertised in the past few years. Their greatest value is in those regions of the country where ice and snow are not a major factor and winters are mild. Many gardeners in the Northeast have enjoyed growing them for limited use because of their attractive appearance, especially those with the yellow-striped foliage.

Neither soil, nor exposure, nor light conditions, are vital factors in growing these plants, but they have special value in shade. Since they make dense, sod-like growth, they need division every few years. They can be reset in fall or spring and require no special care.

Lungwort—6–9″—Zone 3   *Pulmonaria saccharata*

For shady places where the soil does not dry out rapidly, lungwort is a good perennial ground cover. Some gardeners know it as Bethlehem sage. The white-spotted leaves are attractive throughout the season. Pink buds unfold to lovely blue trumpet-shaped flowers in graceful sprays in early spring, before the foliage has fully matured. This plant increases rapidly to make sizable clumps and combines well with other shady perennials, making a pleasing contrast to green tones in the shade because of its mottled foliage. There are several species and improved forms, with flowers ranging from pink to deep blue.

Increase is by division of the creeping rootstock after flowering at any time during the growing season. Ordinary garden soil suits it, but where humus is abundant, it makes great mats of growth rapidly.

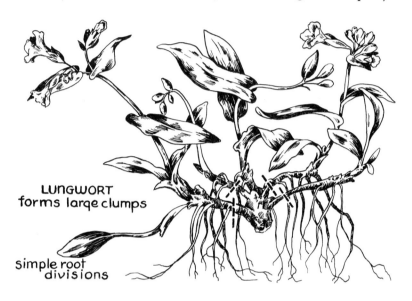

LUNGWORT
forms large clumps

simple root
divisions

Mat Grass—3″—Zone 7   *Lippia canescens*

Mat grass is a southern native found also on the West Coast, used as a lawn substitute. It is sometimes listed as *L. repens* and *Phyla nodiflora*. A fast-growing perennial, it spreads by underground stems which root as they grow. The great value of this plant lies in its ability to tolerate varied conditions of heat and soil and its resistance to salt spray. It forms a dense mat, growing about 3 inches tall in full sun and somewhat higher in shade, and can be mowed and walked upon like grass. Because of its vigorous growth, a heavy stand can be developed in a few months and it has proved to be much more drought-resistant than most lawn grasses.

It is increased by cuttings or sods for more rapid cover. These are set as close as possible for an immediate effect.

Mazus—1″—Zone 5   *Mazus reptans*

A dainty but sturdy matting plant with an easy name, mazus is a rapid-growing ground cover only 1 inch high. Tiny lavender flowers resembling snapdragons stud the leafy rosettes. This plant travels fairly fast over moist soil in partial shade and may become weedy, but it is easy to control because of its shallow root system. It can also become a lawn weed, which may or may not become a problem, depending on the location of its use and the lawn standards you maintain. Its chief merit is its use as a paving plant or for a low mat under taller plants, among rocks or around the edges of pools. The right paving plant for shady places is not always easy to find, but mazus, or creeping veronica (*V. repens*), or creeping mint (*M. requieni*) may well be the answer.

As with many of these creeping alpines, it is easily divided at any season of the year. It prefers moist soil but will grow under average conditions. Adaptable to sun or shade, it seems to prefer subdued light, but even in heavy shade, where little else will grow, it covers the ground.

Moneywort—3"—Zone 3   *Lysimachia Nummularia*

Creeping Jennie, creeping Charlie—it can be called creeping anything, for it is a creeper and a fast one in every sense of the word. It is usually a pest, as are most members of this genus, unless carefully restrained. Yet, the foliage and the flowers of all these plants have many good points in their favor. The fact that many charming folk names are associated with the lysimachias brings to mind the esteem in which they were held in former centuries. This plant covers the ground with leaves that look like small coins attached to the creeping stems. Yellow flowers like buttercups stud the foliage all summer long, sometimes in quantity. It is best suited to moist places in sun or shade. Beginners, often charmed with its rapid growth and easy rooting habit, set it out with great enthusiasm, only to have Jennie or Charlie walk away with the place in no time. Moneywort has its place where needed and it makes the greatest of carpets, with golden blooms to boot. A fellow traveler found with it in gardens is ground ivy or gill-over-the-ground (*Glecoma hederacea*).

It propagates itself and any bit of it with a root moved at any time during the growing season will make its way practically anywhere.

Moss Sandwort—1"—Zone 2   *Arenaria verna caespitosa*

A moss-like alpine about a half-inch high that is widely used as a paving plant, over the greater part of the United States, is often referred to as Irish moss. It is most frequently called moss sandwort or lazy-man's lawn. For many years it was listed as *Sagina subulata* and still appears under this name in some lists and reference books. It can be found growing in almost any well-drained soil except heavy clay, seldom requires clipping, and generally is long-lived. It takes the ordinary foot traffic of gardens without damage and is most useful between flags or paving blocks, for walks, terraces, and patios. When grown in broad masses it occasionally humps up in a mound, but a firm foot puts it back where it belongs. For sunny locations, this and the others listed here also take a fair amount of shade.

A species with a low-creeping, branching habit bearing tiny white cup-shaped flowers in late spring (*A. laricifolia*) does best in sandy acid soil in full sun. Mountain sandwort (*A. montana*), another miniature with glossy foliage, bears large white flowers in late spring on its trailing growth.

Increase of these tiny plants is by division, and most of them have a way of spreading beyond their bounds, providing future supply for places that become worn at times with heavy traffic.

New Zealand Bur—1"—Zone 6 *Acaena microphylla*

These tiny perennials from New Zealand are little known in the colder parts of the Northeast, since their use is limited to areas where winter temperatures are mild. A low, silvery-green creeper that is evergreen, hugging the ground, the rounded leaflets look like miniature burnet foliage. It needs a warm location and full sun. This and several related species are used on the West Coast. A few Eastern dealers offer it.

A plant for neutral or alkaline soils, it can be increased by division. On the tender side, it requires protection north of New York City.

Pachistima—1'—Zone 5 *Pachistima canbyi*

This low, spreading evergreen, which somewhat resembles boxwood in its foliage and texture, though it has been used as a ground cover for more than 50 years is not widely known. Reliably hardy, a native of the mountains of Virginia and the Carolinas, it is at home in rocky soil but grows well under garden conditions where the soil is on the acid side. In full sun it makes denser and more compact growth than in the shade. The small reddish flowers are of little merit in contrast to the handsome foliage on wiry stems, which takes on bronzy tones in autumn.

Use it among rhododendrons or azaleas or with the various broad-leaved evergreens. In foundation plantings, or in areas under windows or wherever a trim year-round appearance is needed, here is an ideal plant, hardy from Massachusetts south. Pachistima is also widely used as a dwarf hedge. A taller-growing species (*P. Myrsinites*) is native to the West Coast.

Propagation is by division of the rooted underground stems or from cuttings. This plant tends to layer naturally and this can be induced by pinning down branches or mounding the soil an inch or two around

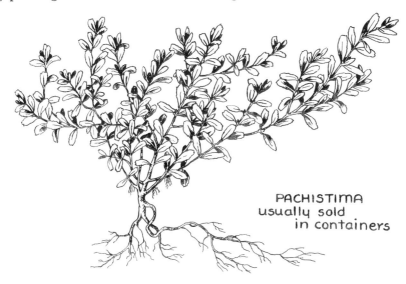

PACHISTIMA
usually sold
in containers

the stems. Prepare soil with ample amounts of peat and organic matter. Small plants from pots or field-grown clumps are easily handled. Rooted cuttings must be handled with care in planting, since they dry out rapidly.

Pachistima adds richness and texture to a planting.

Pachysandra—6″—Zone 4   *Pachysandra terminalis*

Pachysandra, also known as Japanese spurge, is one of the four most widely used ground covers in America. The spoon-shaped leaves, arranged in whorls on trailing stems, make a rippling effect when used in broad carpets. Creamy white spikes of bloom top the foliage in May, and old plants produce whitish fruits in autumn, but these are not common. Easy to grow and propagate, it makes a dense mass for shady areas and grows most satisfactorily even where there is considerable sun. However, it is no plant for hot, dry situations. It burns badly during open winters when planted in exposed areas where wind and sun are its enemies.

Because pachysandra makes a superbly rich green carpet, it fits under such trees as maples and other shallow-rooted kinds which tend to rob the soil of nourishment and make cover of any kind a problem. Interplanted among rhododendrons, azaleas, and other broad-leaved evergreens, it gives a pleasing and finished effect. Along steps on banks and slopes, it serves all the purposes of a good ground cover. It also combines with low-spreading junipers, yews, pieris, leucothoe, and many of the broad-leaved evergreens for equally pleasing effects.

Oftentimes there are shady areas along walks, the sides of houses or garages or other places where it is difficult to maintain grass or other kinds of planting. These are the places for pachysandra. Interest can be added to broad expanses of pachysandra by using low-growing evergreens like dwarf yews, leucothoe, mountain andromeda, Oregon holly-

Maintenance is easy on this shady slope with pachysandra replacing grass.

Pachysandra adds a note of richness to this charming terrace.

grape, and others for accent. The large-leaved plantain-lilies can be used in a similar manner for a contrast in foliage texture.

In recent years a variegated form known as *Silveredge* has been introduced. Lighter green than the type, the leaves are markd with a silvery-white margin, usually ¼ inch or less, outlining each leaf. As with many mottled or variegated foliage plants, *Silveredge* pachysandra supplies a color contrast that brightens broad expanses of green foliage. It can also be used to advantage along margins of broad-leaved evergreen plantings.

A native species known as Allegheny spurge (*P. procumbens*), native from West Virginia to Florida, grows in clumps and is more erect in habit than the familiar Japanese type. Although evergreen in the South, it loses its leaves in northern areas, but the showy spikes of fuzzy white flowers in early spring are very attractive. In regions where it remains evergreen it has some merit, but does not cover so rapidly as *P. terminalis*.

Well-drained soil with plenty of organic material in the form of peat moss, leafmold, or chopped sod gets pachysandra off to a good start. Incorporate fertilizer with the soil when preparing it. An annual top dressing in early spring is also good practice until the area is well covered. After setting out young plants and watering thoroughly, a soil mulch at least 1 inch deep keeps weeds in check. Feeding each spring with a complete fertilizer helps to keep growth vigorous.

Few of our ground covers are as easy to propagate or root more rapidly. Cuttings can be taken after the new growth has formed in early June and rooted in a mixture of sand and peat. An easy way to do this is to prepare a little propagating bed in some corner of your garden under a shrub where you will be sure to water it occasionally. Make the cuttings about 4 inches long with sharp shears. Remove all foliage on that portion of the stem which will be placed in the soil. Usually cuttings root in about 10 days, but they must be kept moist. Sand is also a good medium for rooting pachysandra. Some gardeners simply make cuttings in their own garden soil and shade them until roots appear. Once a good healthy set of roots has developed, the plants can be set out, about 8 to 10 inches apart for intermediate effect. Close planting is worth while with rooted cuttings, to eliminate the job of weeding.

Pachysandra provides an ideal ground cover for rhododendron plantings.

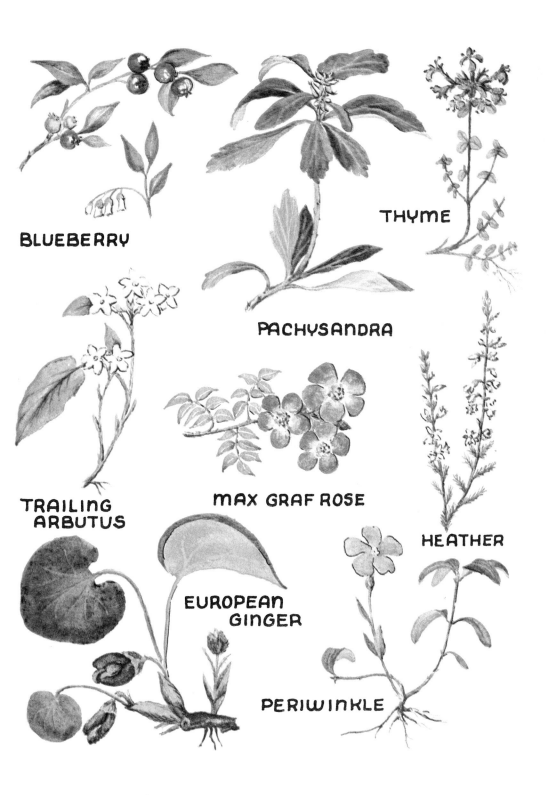

BLUEBERRY

THYME

PACHYSANDRA

TRAILING
ARBUTUS

MAX GRAF ROSE

HEATHER

EUROPEAN
GINGER

PERIWINKLE

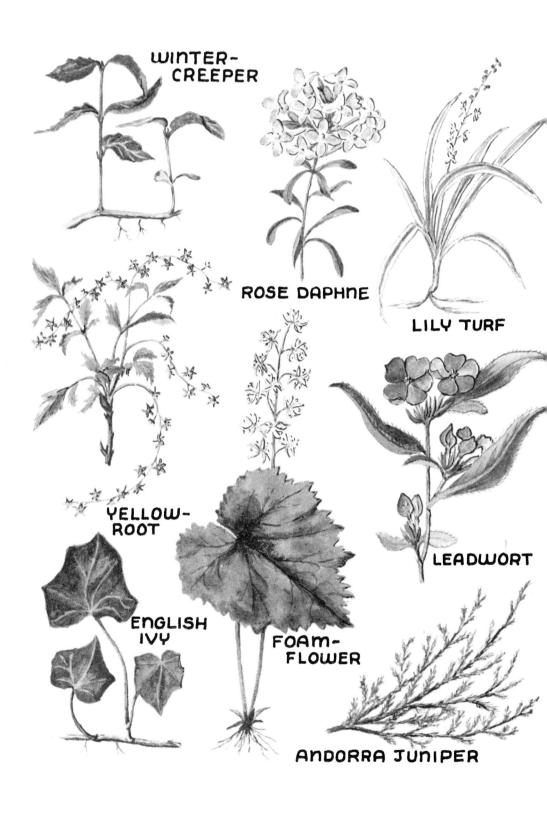

WINTER-CREEPER

ROSE DAPHNE

LILY TURF

YELLOW-ROOT

LEADWORT

ENGLISH IVY

FOAM-FLOWER

ANDORRA JUNIPER

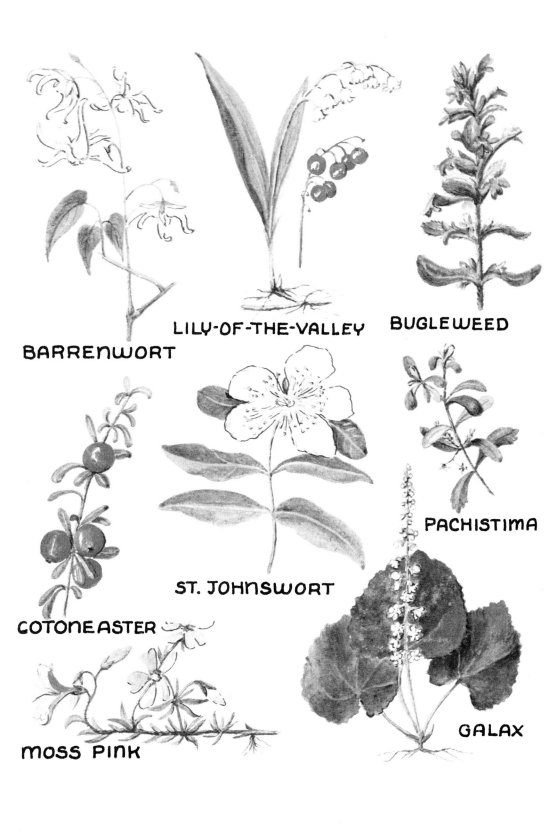

BARRENWORT

LILY-OF-THE-VALLEY

BUGLEWEED

COTONEASTER

ST. JOHNSWORT

PACHISTIMA

MOSS PINK

GALAX

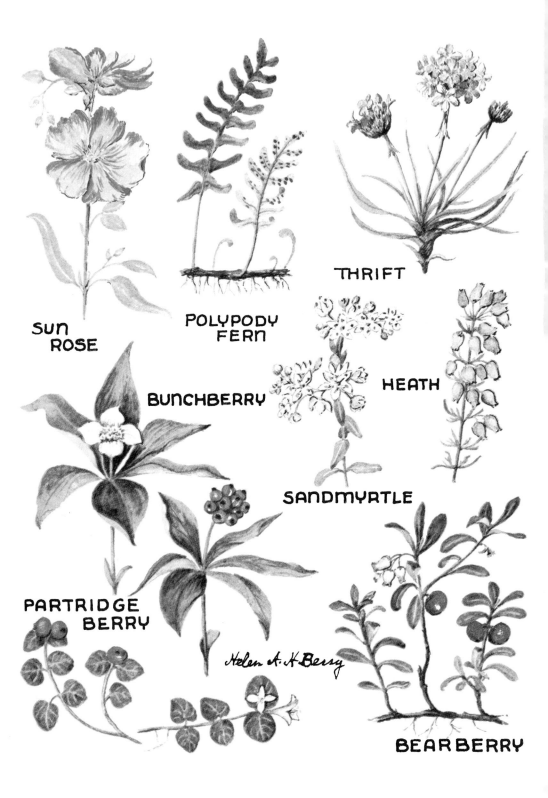

SUN
ROSE

POLYPODY
FERN

THRIFT

BUNCHBERRY

HEATH

SANDMYRTLE

PARTRIDGE
BERRY

Helen A. H Berry

BEARBERRY

Partridge-Berry—2"—Zone 3   *Mitchella repens*

Although not a rugged ground cover nor an easy one to establish, the partridge-berry has uses in woodland plantings, wild gardens, and where its acid-soil requirements and a shady site are available. This native of shady woodlands is found along the entire Eastern seaboard, extending inland to Minnesota and Texas. Part of its appeal lies in its dainty growth of foliage, its miniature flowers, and its showy fruits.

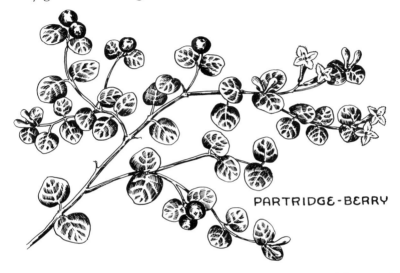

PARTRIDGE-BERRY

The evergreen leaves are white-veined and the fragrant white or pinkish blossoms are borne in pairs, followed by plump red berries ¼ inch in diameter. It is a common sight in the wild to find flowers and fruits appearing at the same time. Because of the delicate tracery it makes, it can be used around imbedded rocks. Often, in wild gardens, it is combined with mosses, rattlesnake plantain, pipsissewa, and other favorites found on the woodland floor. Under cultivation, given acid, humusy soil, partridge-berry spreads to make dense mats, since it roots along its stems as it creeps. Long trailers can be cut back to induce thicker growth. Some care is needed with this native ground cover, but it is always rewarding to succeed in establishing sizable colonies of it on home grounds. It is best moved in sods obtained from a collector, or you can gather your own in the wild, removing as much soil as possible with each sod or mat. Prepare soil with ample amounts of acid leafmold or peat from local sources. If carefully handled, rooted runners can be transplanted, provided that they are kept moist until established. With the present trend toward suburban living and the extensive construction of highways, through wooded areas, it is often possible to obtain plants on land that is to be cleared. It is sound practice to rescue these native plants and set them out in gardens where their requirements for soil and exposure can be met.

Periwinkle—6″—Zone 3 *Vinca minor*

Thomas Jefferson planted periwinkle in his garden at Monticello before the Revolution, and it has been widely used in gardens all over America ever since. In parks, cemeteries, plantings around public buildings, in the city and country wherever gardeners need a green carpet plant, they think immediately of periwinkle or myrtle. Both common names are widely used. It flourishes in sun or shade and is often found in the wild, having escaped from cultivation. Part of the charm of this glossy evergreen trailer lies in its lively blue flowers, which appear in early spring with the daffodils.

The familiar blue-flowering type is *Vinca minor*. There is also a white-flowering variety which is most pleasing. *V. minor atropurpurea* has purple flowers. A double-flowered kind and one with yellow markings on the leaves are sometimes planted. The best of them all is *Bowles* variety, with larger and deeper blue flowers and a more restrained habit of growth than the common periwinkle. It spreads from the expansion of its crown rather than by the rooting of trailing stems, typical of the species.

Big-leaf periwinkle (*V. major*), particularly the variegated form, is frequently seen as a trailer in window boxes and other types of plant containers in various sections of the country. In the South and on the

Periwinkle is a happy solution for this steep slope.

Snowdrops naturalized in a planting of periwinkle.

West Coast this form serves as a ground cover on slopes, sometimes combined with English ivy because its variegated foliage makes a pleasing contrast.

Ordinary soil, well prepared, gives good results in sun or shade. Easy to propagate from division of the clumps or rooted trailers, it can be transplanted at any time of year. When dividing matted clumps, cut back the runners hard to make the rooted portions easy to handle. Otherwise, a newly planted area has a messy appearance. Heavy pruning induces new growth from the rooted portions, which makes for denser cover. Annual feeding of newly planted colonies induces more vigorous growth, as does continued fertilizing of established plantings.

Pinks—3–8"—Zone 2 *Dianthus species*

Hardy pinks are for sunny places where there is ample lime in the soil. We usually think of them as sprawling perennials that are appealing when in flower but a bit untidy afterward, despite their glaucous foliage. However, there are several alpine forms which make enduring mats of blue-green foliage, studded with pink, white, or red fragrant blooms. These are neat of habit, require little care, and give a softening effect to rough, rocky ground and spaces between flagstones or along paths. Not all the rock-garden kinds are rugged enough for ground-cover use, but the various dwarf kinds grown together in a rocky area can be treated effectively as rock or ledge cover.

The maiden pink (*D. deltoides*) makes a blue-green lawn about 3 inches high as it spreads over the ground with masses of bloom ranging from white to deep red in June. From Finland we have the sand pink (*D. arenarius*), with white, fragrant fringed flowers. The cheddar pink (*D. caesius*), its hybrids and other tiny species, and named kinds like *Little Bob, Little Joe,* and *Sammy* make chummy companions to carpet sunny spots.

Average well-drained soil, especially on the gritty side in full sun, is best for pinks used as ground covers. Too much plant food is no asset. Soil on the sweet side improved with lime is essential. They can be propagated by seed, cuttings, or division, but the latter is easiest for most gardeners. Set plants or divisions 10 to 12 inches apart.

Plantain-Lilies—1–3′—Zones 3–5   *Hosta species*

In Victorian times, plantain-lilies were widely used to border perennial beds and shrub borders, or they were grown in shady places and left to themselves to make enormous clumps. Because of their vigor and ease of culture and adaptability to shade, they have been rediscovered by present-day gardeners. They make excellent ground covers under shrubs and trees and in areas where other plants fail to make a presentable appearance. As accent plants, they have few equals among the hardy perennials, since their foliage retains its freshness all season.

Among the plantain-lilies, there are large and small-leaved kinds, some with white margins and others with variegated markings. Blue-green and yellow-green types, as well as some with lustrous dark green foliage, are to be found among the kinds available. For textured effects, for accent, or for striking contrasts with smaller-leaved plants, these plants have value. Flowers are mostly blue, lavender, or purple, but one kind has showy white flowers. Blooms appear from July to September and make an attractive display while they last, but the foliage surpasses them in many ways.

Perhaps the most imposing of all is *H. sieboldiana,* with large broad leaves of notably glaucous coloring, best described as a gray-blue luster. The August or assumption lily, as it is called, *E. plantaginea,* is valued for its polished yellow-green foliage and showy white fragrant flowers in August. Of the variegated sorts, *H. fortunei marginata alba* is outstanding. Leaves are large, glossy, and irregularly margined in white, making a very showy plant often spreading 2 feet or more in diameter. Another variety, *H. viridis marginata,* is yellow-green when it first unfolds, with a subtle edge of darker green, but the contrast is less obvious as summer approaches.

Honeybells, a hybrid plantain-lily.

Plantain-lilies are easy to divide.

Hosta fortunei marginato-alba.

The most widely planted of the small-leaved variegated forms is *H. undulata,* with wavy leaves of light green splashed with creamy-white markings. Of heavier texture and waxy green, *H. undulata univittata* has creamy bands through the centers of the leaves. *H. lancifolia albo-marginata* has a pencil-like, narrow white border on a long, narrow leaf.

Plain green kinds include *H. caerulea, H. erromena,* and *H. lancifolia.* A recent addition to this notable group of plants is a handsome late-blooming kind named *Honeybells,* with spikes of lavender flowers 3 feet or more in height and olive-green foliage.

Plantain-lilies grow in average garden soil in sun or shade. If planted in rich loam they grow to enormous size, especially in shade, for which they are well adapted. One feeding a year in ordinary soil produces good results. Plants are easily divided in spring or fall, or at any time during the growing season. They are completely hardy and seldom affected by pests or diseases.

Plantain-lilies like *Hosta fortunei marginata* are decorative throughout the season.

The August-lily (*H. plantaginea*), one of the showiest, blooms in summer.

(*Above*) Variegated kinds, like *H. undulata*, provide highlights in shady places.

(*Below*) The blue-gray-green foliage of *H. sieboldiana* creates a dramatic accent.

CREEPING AND TRAILING PHLOX

Moss Pink—6″—Zone 2	*Phlox subulata*
Blue Phlox—1′—Zone 3	*Phlox divaricata*
Camla Phlox—8″—Zone 4	*Phlox nivalis*
Mountain Phlox—6″—Zone 4	*Phlox ovata*
Trailing Phlox—6″—Zone 4	*Phlox procumbens*
Creeping Phlox—1′—Zone 4	*Phlox stolonifera*

Low-growing types of phlox are among the most desirable of native hardy perennials for home gardens. They are vigorous, colorful, and permanent, and require little care. Until recent years, they have received far greater attention from British gardeners than in America, their native land. Those listed here have many possibilities for wider use as ground covers in sun and shade.

Rating high on the list as one of the most colorful of all ground covers, *Phlox subulata* has many popular names, such as moss pink, ground pink, creeping phlox, and mountain pink. Its evergreen needle-like foliage makes a desirable mat and the creeping stems develop roots as they spread.

The familiar type, with its magenta flowers, clashes with other colors in the garden, but when used in broad masses with the white form it can be most pleasing. However, there are so many superior varieties in shades of pink, red, lavender, and purple, that there is no point in using the common magenta form. J. Herbert Alexander of Middleboro, Massachusetts, has introduced many of them. Hybrids resulting from crossing *P. subulata* with *P. nivalis* have greatly enlarged the possibilities of use for creeping phlox. Larger blossoms, clearer color, and repeat flowering in the autumn are among the aims of the plant breeders. Improved habits, including denser growth and better winter foliage color, are of prime concern from the point of use as ground covers. The variety *Alexander's Surprise* is valued for its bright pink flowers and its repeat flowering in autumn.

For an inexpensive cover in large rocky areas, creeping phlox is practical and easy to handle. It lends itself to use especially on sloping or hilly terrain. A rapid grower, it is easy to plant, quick to multiply, and thrives in full sun in almost any type of soil, among rocks, on slopes or flat areas. During open winters where zero temperatures are prevalent, it suffers from sun and windburn and has a somewhat ragged appearance which is not the case where there is ample snow cover or in regions where the winters are normally mild. Occasionally plantings become infested with witch grass, which thrives and roots deeply under the foliage of this matting perennial.

Blue phlox (*P. divaricata*), naturalized in a Connecticut country garden.

Similar to *Phlox subulata* in appearance, but somewhat taller and more open in growth, is the trailing phlox (*P. nivalis*). The best-known variety is the lovely *Camla* with salmon-pink blooms 1 inch across. It is not a wild or rampant grower and is ideal for small gardens as a ground cover for limited areas. Rock-garden specialists offer several other outstanding forms introduced by Mrs. J. Norman Henry, noted Pennsylvania plant hunter. Among them is *Gladyn,* a good white with the repeat-flowering habit, but it is tender north of New York City.

Blue phlox and wild Sweet William are common names for *P. divaricata,* one of the fairest blue flowers native to eastern North America. Included in the list of plants which were favorites in the gardens of Williamsburg before the Revolution, it has become increasingly popular during the past few decades. In its native haunts, it is found in thin, moist woodlands, but grows well in average garden soil in sun or part shade. When in blossom, it makes a vivid display in several shades of blue and lavender at tulip time. Although not a dense grower, in the sense that we evaluate ground covers, blue phlox is a filler for use in drifts among ferns, wild flowers, and spring-flowering shrubs and perennials. As generally used in mixed plantings, its cover effect is thin and sparse, but when heavily fed it makes thick mats of growth. Used in broad masses as a background for polyanthus primroses, it makes a delightful combination. There is an improved form called *Laphami,* and a white variety also.

Several species or wild forms of phlox and their hybrids, of interest primarily to wild-garden enthusiasts, are by nature well adapted to ground-cover use and are not as frequently planted as they might be. Mountain phlox (*P. ovata*) makes an open mat of growth with deep purple blooms on stems 1 foot or more tall. Trailing phlox (*P. procumbens*), with flowers in the same range, grows about 6 inches high with rosy-purple color. Several notable hybrids of creeping phlox (*P. stolonifera*), also introduced by Mrs. Henry, have put this phlox in the class of unusual ground covers for places where there is rich, acid soil and shade.

The various kinds of low-growing phlox are of easy culture and free from serious pests. All can be increased by division in early spring or early fall, or at any time during the growing season if they are given the necessary watering after transplanting. Choice kinds can be propagated by cuttings. The native species respond easily to cultivation and make healthier, denser growth if fed annually with a complete fertilizer. These need attention to soil, on the acid side, and are propagated mostly by division.

Primroses and creeping phlox combine happily with wildings and cultivated plants.

Primrose—9″–2′—Zones 4–5   *Primula species*

Primroses are not sturdy ground covers when we compare them with pachysandra, myrtle, ivy, ajuga, and other widely used kinds. Yet, few perennials can surpass them for carpeting effects in spring gardens. They rival the rainbow in their array of color, and the number of their species, varieties, and strains is legion. Light shade or even half-shade gives a longer flowering period and is essential to their survival in summer. Primroses have come to us from the moist meadows of the British Isles, the ravines of the Alps, some from the very roof of the world, and still others from Oriental woodlands.

For bloom in May, in gardens where soil is heavy and naturally moist, colonies of primroses (especially the polyanthus types) fit well under deeply rooted trees and big-scale shrubs. Use them with drifts of the wavy-leaved plantain-lily, a cream-and-green striped form, for contrast in foliage and summer interest. This method of planting is suggested because primrose foliage is often affected by hot weather. The leaves are subject to various chewing insects which disfigure it—a point to remember when choosing a place for primroses. Or, primrose plantings can be augmented also with the small-leaved tuberous-rooted begonias, fancy-leaved caladiums, or trailing fuchsias interplanted between the clumps. These summer-flowering kinds, transplanted from pots, can be set in place without injuring the primrose roots in any way.

Whether you select several kinds or restrict yourself to the most popular group of all, the polyanthus or bunch primroses, they require a fair amount of care. These are not ground covers for easy landscaping by any means. But, with the right location as to soil and shade, growing these carpets can be joy almost unto madness, for this plant family is fascinating and intriguing.

The easiest of all to grow in the average home garden are the polyanthus strains (*P. polyantha*). Individual blooms of exceptional size borne in clusters on sturdy 8-inch stems rise out of clumps of luxurious foliage in May and June. These are adapted to rich, humusy garden soils and tolerate slight acidity, which makes them most adaptable. However, the summer effect of the foliage is not impressive, hence the need for filler plants as mentioned above.

P. sieboldi, a Japanese species, has the characteristics of a good ground cover, since it creeps and spreads by underground runners, but its delicate foliage fades soon after flowering. In May and June the conspicuous clusters of white flowers and those of the pink and purple varieties make a spectacular display. Interplanted with summer-flowering bulbs, its lack of summer foliage will hardly be noticed.

In contrast to most kinds, the auriculas (*P. Auricula*) have rosettes of leathery, evergreen foliage, sometimes glaucous, with showy clusters of

Japanese primroses thrive in moist heavy soil.

Polyanthus primroses make a colorful spring ground cover.

bright flowers in many colors on 6-inch stems, often marked with eyes or rings of contrasting color. Like all the primroses, they need rich humusy soil but with ample amounts of lime mixed in. They are superb among rocks in broad drifts and are amazingly hardy and long-lived if given the best of drainage.

Forms of *P. denticulata* are taller than most of the early kinds, with globular heads of lavender bloom on sturdy stems that begin to flower in early spring, before the soft green rosettes of leaves unfold. The foliage is usually very durable through the summer. No lime is needed for this acid lover.

The Japanese primroses (*P. japonica*) are among the most striking members of the tribe, with their bright red, pink, or purple flowers arranged in whorls of several tiers. The bloom spikes of the Japanese primroses reach 18 inches or more in height, standing well above the rosettes of leaves from which they emerge. They have deep, fibrous roots, need all the moisture possible, and are ideal stream-side or bog plants. Flowering starts in late May and extends to early summer. Acid, peaty soil on the moist side keeps them happy in sunny locations. In average moist garden soil, give them at least half-shade.

P. juliae hybrids are dwarf in habit, to 3 inches, with flowers emerging a few inches higher from the rosettes of foliage, holding one or several blooms on wiry stems in May. Moist soil and partial shade in most gardens will bring them through successfully.

Soil requirements and light conditions as indicated for the various species are of vital importance for continued success with primroses. They can be increased by dividing the clumps after flowering or in late summer. Thorough soil preparation with ample amounts of humus in the form of leafmold and peat moss, or both, is the easiest way to a good start. Annual feeding pays dividends. All of these primroses can be raised from seed—a challenging venture for the beginner. During open winters, plants may tend to heave, especially when grown on sloping ground or where they are exposed to winter sun. Periods of alternate thawing and freezing can damage them. A mulching around the crowns and a cover of evergreen boughs serve as good insurance.

Pussytoes—1–2″—Zone 3 *Antennaria rosea*

An alpine from the Rocky Mountains of mat-like habit, it makes miniature evergreen rosettes of silvery texture that hug the ground. White flowers appear in early summer, but it is the attractive foliage and the adaptability of this little plant to thrive in full sun and sandy soil that make it useful. Because of its slow-growing habit, it is easy to handle. A faster-growing kind is *A. neodioica,* with fuzzy rose-pink flowers and similar glistening foliage, also evergreen. Another species, *A. rosea,* has pink bloom with the same type of foliage and growing habit. These are plants for filling spaces between and along the sides of stepping stones or flat paved surfaces in full sun.

These tiny plants root as they run and are easy to increase by clipping small bits from plants to increase your stock. Several similar species are included in discussing crevice plants, since not all are available in any one region of the country. Rock-garden specialists are the easiest and most reliable sources of these tiny plants.

Rock Soapwort—6″—Zone 2 *Saponaria ocymoides*

A bright and showy alpine, rock soapwort forms broad, spreading mats of deep pink flowers in late spring, lasting nearly a month. It is well suited to rocky sites in full sun, where it can scramble and cover sizable areas, once planted. This perennial has a tendency to self-sow and is valued for its hardiness. Because of its soft, rapid growth, it often needs to be cut back after flowering in order to produce fresh foliage for a tidy appearance.

Rock soapwort, with its cerise bloom, makes a show for several weeks in spring.

Full sun and ordinary well-drained garden soil are all it needs. It is easily grown from seed, but plants of any size are most difficult to transplant because of the long, tap-like root. Self-sown seedlings are usually plentiful and easy to handle when small.

Rose Daphne—12″—Zone 4 *Daphne Cneorum*

Imagine a ground cover of this fragrant, handsome trailing evergreen—it just can't be, you think. Yet, in its native home, this procumbent shrub makes a mat often yards long. But in many gardens it languishes because of damage from winter sun and wind, especially when there is little or no snow cover. During the winter in areas of zero temperature, it needs a protective covering of evergreen branches, and it is well worth the trouble. The bright pink flowers, borne in clusters above the gray-green foliage, are delightfully fragrant. Peak of its flowering is late April and May, but it often sends forth stray bloom again in late summer. Except in sizable gardens, one would not expect to see it in large, broad masses, but several plants grouped together can make a

Rose daphne often needs winter cover to prevent sunburned foliage.

mass to create a memorable effect as a foreground planting for broad-leaved evergreens. It shows to best advantage on a slight slope, or among rocks.

Well-drained sandy soil in full sun or light shade suits it best. Add plenty of organic material, including peat, when you plant it, and give it a mulch of peat moss. This dwarf shrub resents disturbance and it is important to get freshly dug balled and burlapped or container-grown specimens. Feed with evergreen fertilizer in early spring and avoid cultivation around the roots. Mulch with peat moss or oak leaves, since the garland flower is accustomed to a moist root run in its natural habitat. For ground-cover effects, set plants 30 inches apart. Annual shearing of plants until they make a dense mat is good practice. This is best done after flowering and before mid-July so that the new growth will mature before cold weather.

TRAILING ROSES

Creeping Rugosa Rose—1″—Zone 4	*Rosa rugosa alba*
Memorial Rose—1″—Zone 5	*Rosa wichuraiana*
Trailing Hybrid Roses—1″—Zone 5	*Rosa hybrids*

Roses as ground covers have many points in their favor where they can be used to advantage on the home grounds. Attractive foliage, colorful and often fragrant bloom (sometimes everblooming), showy fruits with some kinds, vigorous growth—these are among their assets. Add to these the fact that they are thorny and you include the element of protection from trespassing. Certain of our large-flowered climbing roses, not generally thought of as suited to trailing, have been adapted for use on banks and slopes to create striking landscape effects. In areas of extremely low winter temperatures, a number of climbers are brought into bloom only by growing them on the ground.

Among the climbing roses there are two distinct groups for general ground-cover use: the ramblers and the trailing, or creeping, varieties. Scrambling over ledges or rocky areas, mass-planted on slopes or steep banks within the grounds or along boundaries, flanking steps to various levels—these are typical ways to use ramblers and trailing roses.

The rambler roses, of which *Dorothy Perkins* and *Crimson Rambler* are the two best known, have lost favor with gardeners because they are subject to mildew in most gardens.

Best known of the trailing roses are *Max Graf* and the *Memorial Rose.* These have been widely used as ground covers for nearly a half-century. During the past two decades, the late W. D. Brownell of Little Compton, Rhode Island, developed many notable trailing or creeping varieties which have become popular wherever roses are grown. They are noted for their vigor, the excellence of their color, and their hardiness. To see them is to want to find a place for them. Many are included in the following list.

The Brownell creeping roses are ideal ground covers for large areas.

Apricot Glow. Fragrant, double apricot-pink flowers in June. This trailer is valued for its bloom, its glossy foliage, and its vigor.

Carpet of Gold. One of many outstanding climbers developed by the Brownells. Shiny, vigorous foliage with double yellow, fragrant blossoms in clusters.

Cherokee Rose. A single white fragrant rose, borne on sturdy evergreen growth, it is the state flower of Georgia. Tender in the North, it is seen frequently in Florida, in the deep South, and on the West Coast.

Creeping Everbloom. A double 4-inch red hybrid-tea-type rose, it is free-flowering, recurrent in its bloom and fragrant.

Crimson Shower. A recently introduced hybrid of the rugged *Memorial Rose* with clusters of clear crimson bloom from July to late summer.

Ever-Blooming Yellow Climber. This is another of Mr. Brownell's valuable roses. The semi-double yellow blossoms are fragrant and can be counted on for repeat bloom.

Golden Glow. Large bright yellow blooms with tea fragrance in June and July, and leathery foliage, are the notable features of this variety.

Little Compton Creeper. Single, bright wild-rose-pink flowers in loose clusters, this is a superb variety with glossy foliage and colorful vermilion fruits in autumn. Not quite so flat as some others, it grows at a slight angle, making a memorable display.

Max Graf. Single pink flowers with showy golden stamens, it has rugged rugosa-type foliage. Unlike most roses, it tolerates considerable shade, is completely hardy and a vigorous grower. It is one of the oldest and most widely planted roses for ground cover.

Memorial Rose. This is actually *Rosa wichuraiana,* a species native to the Orient. The single white, fragrant blossoms, accentuated by showy yellow stamens, appear in early summer. Canes root when covered with soil, making it a valuable bank cover.

Mermaid. Visitors to rose gardens are often intrigued when they see the handsome single rose *Mermaid* growing on banks, holding its superb large single flowers, often measuring 5 to 6 inches across, against a mass of glossy foliage that makes a very handsome display.

Pink Cherokee. Fragrant, single, deep pink blossoms appear all summer on this rampant grower, which is a favorite in the South. A tender rose, it is not suited to cold climates.

Red Cherokee (Ramona). This is a sport of the *Pink Cherokee* with light crimson flowers all summer that fade to a softer pink and are fragrant.

Rosa rugosa repens alba. This creeping form of the rugosa rose is not grown too widely, but it deserves considerable attention from gardeners faced with the problem of ground covers in poor, sandy soils by the seashore or elsewhere. The white flowers are followed by showy red hips.

White Banksia. This is the *Lady Banks* rose of the South, also widely grown in California. A rampant grower with large clusters of tiny flowers, it has the fragrance of violets. There are single and double forms, and a yellow variety.

Plant these trailing types as you would any rose, by digging a generous hole and preparing the soil with plenty of plant food and good garden soil. Water thoroughly and give them a temporary mound of soil until the roots are set. On steep inclines, a pocket of soil around each plant to catch water and a mulch to keep the soil from washing out the roots are good practice. They require little care except occasional pruning to remove canes that tend to grow upright and those that extend themselves beyond the limits set for them. Plants can be planted bare-root in spring or fall or from containers at any time during the growing season.

Trailing rose *Max Graf* performs well even in part shade.

St. John's-Wort—18″—Zones 4–6   *Hypericum species*

The St. John's-worts are showy, low-growing shrubs found native in various parts of the United States and Europe. They have soft, light green foliage and thrive in full sun, but make a good display in a fair amount of shade. Showy yellow tassel-like blooms appear over a long period in summer, and plants require no special soil or attention. Nurserymen on both sides of the Atlantic have turned their attention to these showy plants in recent years, and several improved forms have been featured in catalogs. Some kinds are known to rock-garden enthusiasts and others are collected by those who grow dwarf shrubs. The St. John's-worts make good ground covers of varying heights and are most adaptable as well as decorative, but some of them cannot be

Glaucous foliage and yellow tassel-like flowers of St. John's-wort.

counted on for hardiness in areas of prolonged sub-zero temperatures without benefit of snow cover.

A species native to the Blue Ridge Mountain region, *H. bucklei,* less than 1 foot tall, bears its yellow tassels in June. One plant makes a mat of soft foliage a yard wide, and, while not evergreen, is most desirable. *H. calycinum,* listed in many catalogs, grows 1 foot to 18 inches tall and spreads by underground stems, making a mat of glaucous foliage which is evergreen, or partially so, depending on the winter temperature.

A taller-growing species, *H. moserianum,* reaches 2 feet in height and is known as gold flower. Even when it dies back to the ground, it makes rapid new growth and blooms freely in July and August. A creeping form, *H. repens,* is a low-growing kind, 6 to 8 inches tall, with showy bloom in early summer. The new variety *Sungold,* patented in recent years, grows 1½ to 2 feet tall and spreads twice as wide, with an abundance of golden-yellow flowers throughout the summer. *Hidcote* grows nearly twice as tall in moderate climates but, even where it dies back to the ground, it flowers freely on the current season's growth.

Well suited to sandy soils in full sun or light shade, plants are listed by many nurseries throughout the country. Container-grown plants are easy to plant at any season of the year. Stock may be increased by cuttings, segments of the rooted stems, division, or seed, according to the types grown.

Sand Myrtle—15″—Zone 4   *Leiophyllum buxifolium*

All too little known, sand myrtle, with its glossy box-like foliage borne on open, irregular, wiry branches, makes a billowy evergreen mass of miniature growth that is attractive throughout the year. Native from New Jersey to Florida, it thrives under the same conditions as the heaths and heathers and makes a fitting companion for them. Although full sun suits it best, it will do well in part shade. Pink buds in clusters unfold as fuzzy star-like white flowers appear in May and June. During the cold months the enduring foliage takes on a bronzy cast. In addition to the typical form, there is a compact variety known as Allegheny sand myrtle (*L. lyoni*), which hugs the ground, 6 to 8 inches tall. Both types, depending on the height desired, are suited for large pockets of acid soil among rocks and ledges.

Obtain balled and burlapped or container-grown plants and set them out in well-prepared sandy, acid soil, using leafmold and peat, spacing them 1 foot apart. Feed with evergreen fertilizer and water frequently until the plants are established. This is not an easy plant to establish, but the record of success with it is most gratifying.

Sand myrtle and cotoneaster scrambling over a rock.

Sarcococca—1–2′—Zone 5   *Sarcococca humilis*

Among the lesser-known plants used for ground cover in recent years is a choice, low-growing, broad-leaved evergreen with the awkward name *Sarcococca hookeriana humilis,* native to the Himalaya Mountains. It is sometimes referred to as sweet-box, a pleasant way to remember a charming plant and much easier to recall than small Himalayan sarcococca. The foliage is like that of leucothoe, only smaller, glossy in appearance and leathery in texture. Clusters of small, white fragrant blooms appear along the stems in early spring, followed by black berries. Growth is usually 1 to 2 feet tall, depending on the soil, the location, and the climate. It spreads by underground rootstocks, making dense clumps when well established.

Grown under rhododendrons and azaleas or used in broad masses in shady locations, it has refined and pleasing habit. Not hardy where zero temperatures are of long duration, it nonetheless has been grown successfully beyond its supposed northern limits of southern New England. In the Northwest and in northern California it is used to great advantage.

An acid-soil plant, it prefers rich, peaty soil and a shady location. Prepare the soil carefully when planting and water frequently until it is well established. Propagation is by division of the creeping rootstocks and by cuttings.

Savory—Zones 5–7   *Satureia species*

The name savory brings to mind a flavoring herb used to give zest to meats and other foods, but there are several species that make admirable cover plants. These are dwarf shrubs native to Europe which are grown over a large part of the country in rock and herb gardens. Little thought has been given to their use as ground covers in rocky, sandy soil for hot, dry situations.

Calamint (*S. calamintha*) is a creeper only a few inches high with pungent leaves and purple flowers from late spring through midsummer. The species *S. globella,* listed by rock-garden specialists, is even more dwarf in habit and ideally suited to terraces and paths. A native of Kentucky, its flowers are tiny purple bells on 3-inch stems. West Coast gardeners use yerba buena (*Micromeria chamissoni,* formerly listed as a savory) for a ground cover now, although the early settlers considered it primarily as a valuable herb with a pleasing minty fragrance. Stems often trail 2 feet or more, bearing tiny white flowers. Winter savory (*S. montana*) is a tall-growing kind, to 15 inches, with tiny lavender flowers in summer. The forms *S. montana pygaea* and *S. montana subspicata* are compact forms, less than 6 inches tall.

Full sun and gritty soil are the easy requirements for savory. Division or cuttings are the methods home gardeners use to increase their stock. Many kinds can be raised from seed.

Silver Mound Artemisia—4–12″—Zone 3   *Artemisia schmidtiana*

The nation's largest nursery catalog lists this plant as Silver Mound Artemisia, and well-named it is. It grows with great vigor in full sun and poor soil and makes handsome mounds of silvery, finely cut foliage which are eye-catching all season long. Often used singly in small rock gardens or as an edging for wide borders, it shows off to equally good advantage as a ground cover in rocky areas or on slight slopes. A tall-growing type, a foot or more in height, and the dwarf *A. schmidtiana nana* are both desirable. In fact, the latter is often desired for its low growth. Other species of this hardy and vigorous tribe of perennials include fringed wormwood (*A. frigida*), 15 to 18 inches tall, and the rather weedy Roman wormwood (*A. pontica*), common in old gardens. All have inconspicuous yellow flowers, but the great charm of these plants is their foliage and the ease with which they grow. Every garden needs silvery foliage for accent. This group of artemisias has many uses, especially for mass effects.

SILVER MOUND
ARTEMISIA

Division of clumps is the way to increase stock. Artemisias spread rapidly and are easy to divide at any time during the growing season. If Silver Mound gets shoddy with too much rain, causing the mounds to open, cut it back and watch it quickly send up new growth.

The silvery-gray foliage of snow-in-summer is an added asset.

Snow-in-Summer—6″—Zone 2   *Cerastium tomentosum*

If we accept the simple definition of a weed as a plant out of place, then snow-in-summer fits that category. Yet, when used where it is needed, it can be the handsomest of ground covers through most of the year. It came into gardens as a plant for rock and wall gardens and it truly is at home among the crevices of rocks in hot, dry situations. The gray woolly foliage makes dense mats studded with starry white flowers in May and June. It covers sizable areas in a short time and keeps down weeds satisfactorily. If it becomes messy in appearance as a result of tramping or animal damage, shear it back to encourage new growth. The same treatment holds for browning, which occurs with too much wet weather followed by extreme dry spells. Snow-in-summer is practically indestructible and self-sows readily, but it can be kept under control. Gardeners with difficult rocky sites or banks to be covered in a hurry make the most of this easy perennial. When it outgrows its space or its usefulness, yank it out.

Division of clumps in early spring or fall, or at any season of the year, and the use of seedling plants, are the usual methods of increase. Poor soil and full sun satisfy its needs.

Speedwell—Zones 3–5   *Veronica species*

In the heyday of perennial gardens and during the years when rock gardening was all the rage, many species and varieties of veronica, or speedwell, as it is commonly known, were listed in catalogs. Many kinds have blue flowers of good color, and there are pink forms, but they are not spectacular as are some perennials. Yet, they are of easy culture, have clean, persistent foliage, and are practically disease-free. Among them are many dwarf kinds admirably suited to ground-cover use, ranging in height from a few inches to 1 foot or more, including the flower spikes. Some nurseries list a few, but most rock-garden specialists grow them in wide variety.

To gardeners who take pride in their lawns and wage a continual battle against carpeting weeds, mention of creeping speedwell (*V. repens*) makes them shudder. They know it as a mean weed. It thrives in shade, makes a tight, flat mat of glossy foliage that roots as it creeps. It is most useful as a paving plant in shade. Pale blue flowers in spring add to its appearance. Another weedy species is *V. filiformis,* with bright blue-and-white flowers, nearly evergreen in its matting foliage, and most appealing when in flower. A good paving plant, some gardeners use it as an undercover for primroses. Other kinds for paving and crevice use are *V. armena,* with lacy evergreen foliage and vivid blue flowers, for shady locations, and *V. pectinata,* with woolly evergreen leaves for sunny places. A variety of this species has pink flowers.

Taller-growing kinds include the woolly speedwell (*V. incana*), valued for its silvery foliage only 4 inches high and brilliant blue flower spikes rising some 6 inches taller. There is a pink form also. Germander speedwell (*V. Chamaedrys*) is an evergreen type with excellent matting foliage. Flowers are blue or white, according to the variety.

These are among the better kinds which can be used in broad masses in full sun or light shade for colorful flowers during spring and early summer.

As a group, the speedwells are of the easiest culture in ordinary garden soil in full sun or light shade. All are easily divided in spring or fall. They transplant readily and require a minimum of care.

Creeping veronicas are useful to soften edges of steps and paved areas.

The cheery pink bloom of stone cress looks like rose daphne.

Stone Cress—6″—Zone 3   *Aethionema warleyense*

Like arabis and aubrieta, this alpine shrub, known as Persian candytuft, forms compact mounds of gray-blue needle-like leaves studded with deep pink flower heads in May and June. Free-flowering and long-lasting, this miniature shrub reminds one of a small edition of rose daphne. Well suited to rocky areas, used in broad masses or combined with other alpines, it is a truly delightful plant for limited use as a ground cover.

Full sun and gritty soil well mixed with lime are its requirements. Propagate by division or cuttings. Shearing after flowering improves the growth and makes it denser. Stone chips make a good mulch for this native of the Mediterranean. Sun and wind damage are likely in open winters and present more of a problem than hardiness.

Stonecrop—3–12″—Zone 2   *Sedum species*

Mention stonecrops or sedums to most gardeners and they shout "weeds" or "pests," for some of them are precisely that. Yet, where soil cover is needed in sun or light shade and large areas are involved, sedums are often the answer. On stony locations, on slopes or banks, or among ledges where soil is sparse, the sturdy stonecrops have a place. Because of their shallow roots, they are easy to eradicate when they attempt to run away with any given area. Low-growing, free-flowering, and requiring little care, they are often of great use, especially at summer places where low maintenance is essential.

Sedum acre, sometimes called mossy stonecrop, actually grows by the acre in a short time. One of the lowest-growing of all, 2 to 3 inches, its flowers make a carpet of gold above miniature evergreen foliage. A white-flowering form which grows twice as tall (*S. album*), also makes a good matting plant. *S. lydium* is another white form. Stringy stonecrop (*S. sarmentosum*) produces its yellow flowers in early summer on stems about 6 inches tall. The so-called two-row stonecrop (*S. spurium*) makes mats of dense growth, is partially evergreen in mild climates, and flowers in midsummer with pink flowers fading to white.

Not all the sedums can be considered as commonplace and weedy. Because of their ability to flourish in hot, dry situations, hybridizers have developed some notable improved forms. *S. spurium* is the source

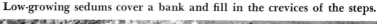

Low-growing sedums cover a bank and fill in the crevices of the steps.

of a rich red kind known as *Dragon's Blood*. It flowers from July on and the general effect is one of varying shades of red from the bronzy tones of buds and stems to the carmine flowers which fade to crimson. The species *S. sieboldi*, with its rounded silvery-gray leaves edged with red, grows like a great flat rosette, bearing bright pink flowers in September on gracefully curved stems. *Capablanca*, a form of *S. spathulifolium*, has blue-green foliage topped with flat heads of yellow bloom in late spring. In variety, they are legion and in the proper places are well worth growing.

Ordinary dry soil, even on the poor side, suits all the stonecrops. The smallest bit with a root will grow, and they can stand drought and neglect with ease.

STRAWBERRIES AND THEIR RELATIVES

American Strawberry—6–10″—Zone 3	*Fragaria vesca americana*
Sand Strawberry	*Fragaria chiloensis*
Virginia Strawberry	*Fragaria virginiana*
Wood Strawberry	*Fragaria californica*
Barren Strawberry	*Waldsteinia fragarioides*
Mock Strawberry	*Duchesnea indica*

Our wild strawberries and their relatives are natural ground covers. The early New England settlers considered them manna from heaven as they pounced upon the ripe berries they found among the grasses on a June morning more than three centuries ago. "The best I have ever eaten," wrote Governor John Winthrop in his diary. They are still good eating and much more flavorsome than some of the enormous spongy berries we buy in the market.

Both the Virginia and the American strawberry are native over a large part of the northern and southern portions of the country. On the West Coast, the sand strawberry, one of the parents of our edible garden varieties, is prevalent in sunny areas in the wild. Its counterpart in shade is the wood strawberry, with thinner and lighter green foliage. All have showy white flowers and foliage that is partially evergreen, increase by runners which make dense mats, and have red, tasty fruit. These are assets enough for any cover plant. In cultivation, when planted closely, they make a richly textured carpet. For good results they require care, but it is routine and worth the effort. They fill the bill as appropriate ground covers around historic sites and in Colonial gardens. Try them under high-branched trees and big-scale shrubs, on low banks or in woodland gardens and in formal areas, where they have sun at least half the day. Strawberries make a foliage pattern that looks like a green tapestry.

Related kinds include the mock or Indian strawberry (*Duchesnea indica*), an Asiatic plant that has become widely naturalized along the East Coast. It is easily recognized by its characteristic foliage and flowers of typical form, only yellow. A most desirable cover plant, it is listed by a number of nurserymen. Florists have long used it in basketwork because of its pleasing appearance. The barren or dry strawberry (*Waldsteinia fragarioides*) is noted for its glossy foliage which turns a bronzy purple in autumn and is still conspicuous when the shiny leaves are unfolding in spring. Yellow blossoms about ½ inch in diameter, appearing in May and June, add to its beauty. Both kinds do well in sun or light shade.

A species listed as *F. darwini* is found in some catalogs. Other kinds include *Baron Solemacher,* which forms rapid-growing clumps without runners and is easily raised from seed. Another short-lived kind without runners is Hautbois (*F. moschata*). This and its yellow-fruited variety are not common. There are various yellow- and white-fruited forms of the wild strawberry which some gardeners enjoy growing.

Wild strawberries grow easily in both acid and alkaline soils. Full sun or part shade suit them. For good growth and a dense cover, prepare and fertilize the soil as for any perennial. Stock is increased by division of clumps or by the rosettes of leaves which appear on the runners. Set them a foot apart or closer to make rapid cover. Annual feeding and watering in dry spells keeps strawberry carpets in flourishing condition. Most gardeners prefer to collect their own selected kinds in the wild. Strawberries are shallow-rooted and sometimes the plants heave in open winters. A cover of evergreen boughs serves as protection—a practical way to make use of Christmas trees in January.

Baron Solemacher strawberry is easily raised from seed.

Strawberry Geranium—3″—Zone 6   *Saxifraga sarmentosa*

Strawberry geranium or strawberry begonia and mother-of-thousands are common names for an old-time house plant widely grown as a ground cover in the South and on the West Coast. It is neither a begonia nor a geranium, but these names have been attached to it because of its foliage, and the runners by which it increases resemble those of the strawberry. It has been known to survive in sheltered spots in the Boston area and makes a most charming carpet plant in moist, shady places where the soil is acid. Along paths, between rocks, for terrace plantings where it can trail, or under taller plants, it is at home. Rounded leaves with scalloped edges, blotched white, form a compact rosette from which thread-like trailing stems emerge, forming smaller rosettes. A little gem, it sends forth feathery sprays of white or pink flowers 6 inches to 1 foot tall in June. It is practically evergreen.

Easy to increase by division or by the rooted rosettes, it requires no special attention except a protected location where zero temperatures occur in winter.

Sun-Rose—8″—Zone 5   *Helianthemum Nummularium*

Sun-rose is the common name for various dwarf shrubs known as helianthemums. They are often used in rock gardens, and because of their evergreen character and low-spreading habit they are useful for covering soil. They belong in sunny locations, among rocks, on slopes or flat areas, and endure dryness with ease. Yet, they can take considerable moisture as long as drainage is adequate. They are of somewhat loose habit and are casual in their billowy effect; the pointed, oval leaves may be glossy or silvery, according to variety. Usually they average 6 to 8 inches in height and spread to 3 feet or more in width. There are many bright colors among the hybrids, but the individual cup-shaped flowers last only a day. They are long-lived and vigorous and, like many dwarf-flowering shrubs, benefit from shearing after the flowering period. They prefer a limey soil and are hardy without damage where snow cover is ample. Evergreen boughs for shading are often needed to eliminate windburn where winters are open and temperatures go to zero or below.

These plants resent disturbance and need to be planted as small rooted cuttings from containers. Avoid cultivation and apply lime annually. Give them full sun. Shearing after first flowering induces new growth for a second bloom.

Sweet Woodruff—6–8″—Zone 4   *Asperula odorata*

A neat little perennial with its leaves arranged in whorls on squarish stems, sweet woodruff carries its tiny four-pointed white stars at the tips of the whorls and blooms for many weeks in early spring. It prospers in average garden soil and is most vigorous when there is ample humus content. Spreading by underground stems, it makes a mat of even height. Gardeners who grow it will tell you that its foliage when crushed and cut has the fragrance of new-mown hay and vanilla, and that it is used in wine drinks in Germany and Austria, among them the May wine. A most useful shady ground cover under high-branched evergreens like spruce, fir, and pine, planted along shady garden paths or under such broad-leaved shrubs as rhododendrons and others that have shallow root systems, it proves most satisfactory. The tiny species daffodils coming up through mats of sweet woodruff are always delightful. Almost every garden has a place for a patch of it.

Easy to increase by division of the creeping stems at any time during the garden year, this is a most satisfactory perennial to handle.

Sweet woodruff is valued for its dainty texture and dense growth.

The tufted clumps of thrift can be used to make a pattern.

Thrift—4–10″—Zone 1   *Armeria maritima*

Thriving in most soils except heavy loam, thrift is one of the easiest of ground covers to grow and increase in hot, dry locations inland or by the sea. Among rocks, in sandy, gritty soils, on slopes or flat ground, wherever there is good drainage, this tufted plant grows with ease. At iris time and for a month following, the grasslike mounds are studded with pink, bell-shaped flowers on wiry stems held well above the foliage. Common thrift (*Armeria maritima*) has magenta-pink flowers, while the improved form, *A. maritima laucheana,* native to Greenland, has bright carmine flowers in May with occasional bloom throughout the summer. The variety *Six Hills* is more dwarf, more compact than the type with light pink flowers. Thrift makes a desirable companion for heaths and heathers as a mixed ground cover.

Easy to handle, clumps can be divided at any time during the growing season, setting the divisions 8 inches apart. It can be used to make a pattern planting over a large area by setting clumps 1 foot or more apart and mulching the areas between with crushed stone or pebbles. As the cushion-like growth expands in size, it sometimes browns in the centers, an indication that it needs dividing.

A thyme lawn in a seaside garden spills over the steps.

Thyme, Mother-of-Thyme—2–4"—Zone 2   *Thymus Serpyllum*

Thyme is a plant never forgotten once it has been stepped upon.
Kings and warriors, noblemen and peasants down through the centuries
have grown it, used it for flavoring, and trodden on it. Bees love it and
honey from its jewel-like flowers is a delight. This carpet plant has
many forms, both species and varieties, but most useful of all for a
flat cover are forms of *T. Serpyllum,* known as mother-of-thyme. There
are white, lavender, crimson, and reddish-purple flowered varieties,
one with white margins and another with yellow coloring in its leaves.
Lemon thyme has yellow-green foliage and woolly thyme is just what
its name says, grayish in texture.

A green rug for slight slopes, a covering among rocks, dry walks, and
ledges, a crevice plant for walls and terraces and for uneven ground
surfaces, thyme is at its best in the sun. Several kinds, or as many as
you can collect, will make a bank that you will enjoy working about.
The common thyme (*T. vulgaris*) makes a broad, shrubby mound 6
inches or more in height and the hairy-stemmed kind (*T. lanicaulis*)
makes a down-covered mound of pinkish-lavender loam, 6 inches high
and many times as wide. There are many other kinds, some carpeting
and others shrubby, all worth growing.

A hot, dry, rocky soil on the poor side where the sun shines all day
is the best place for thyme. Since the smallest portion with a root will
grow, there is no need to start it from seed unless the aim is to grow
some species not easily available. Thyme likes lime, but grows in acid
soil.

Trailing Arbutus—3"—Zone 3   *Epigaea repens*

Trailing arbutus, the state flower of Massachusetts, called mayflower
in New England, is one of the most talked-about wild flowers among
growers of native plants. To succeed with it and to propagate trailing
arbutus successfully is considered an achievement. Found on the borders
of woodlands or sometimes on hillsides, it makes a brave show in early
spring in the Northeast as the snow recedes. This ground cover is native from Newfoundland to Florida.

In "Nature's Garden," Neltje Blanchan has recorded the charm
of this plant and the sentiment attached to it. "Can words describe the
fragrance of the very breath of spring—that delicious commingling of
the perfume of arbutus, the odor of pines, and the snow-soaked soil
just warming into life? Those who know the flower only as it is sold
in the city streets, tied with wet, dirty string into tight bunches,

withered and forlorn, can have little idea of the joy of finding the pink, pearly blossoms freshly opened among the withered leaves of oak and chestnut, moss, and pine needles in which they nestle close to the cold earth in the leafless, windy northern forest. Even in Florida, where broad patches carpet the woods in February, one misses something of the arbutus's accustomed charm simply because there are no slushy remnants of snow drifts, no reminder of winter hardships in the vicinity."

Trailing arbutus is truly an untamed wilding. Extremely difficult to transplant and perpetuate, a few specialists propagate plants from cuttings to satisfy the demands of wild-flower gardeners and others interested in this choice native plant. It is a true ground cover, since it spreads by creeping stems, but it is comparatively rare in cultivation. Choosing the site for it is not always as difficult as transplanting it. Unless a colony of arbutus is known to be in the path of progress and is doomed to destruction, it is not in the best interests of conservation to dig this plant. In the wild it is found in gravelly, acid soil and its location may be sun or shade.

A slow grower, it makes only a few inches of cover each year. Since its delicate root system is easily injured, it needs careful handling. Sods or potted plants obtained from nurseries specializing in wild flowers are best for the home garden. Select a semi-shaded location on a slight slope and prepare the soil to be a sandy mixture of acid substance. A mulch of partially decayed oak leaves or pine needles to prevent loss of moisture is good practice. Newly set plants need frequent watering until they are well established.

Trillium—1'—Zone 2   *Trillium species*

Wakerobins or trilliums are of many kinds and make gardening in the shade a joy. When grown in masses they make a display of great beauty, particularly the large-flowered white wakerobin (*T. grandiflorum*), whose blossoms turn pink with age. In open spaces of moist woodland they carpet the ground with lush foliage and showy flowers in May and June. Mingling with them you will find the mayapples, spring beauty, anemones, wild phlox, and other favorites. The blossoms of the purple trillium (*T. erectum*), in the brown-purple to maroon category, are rich indeed, but less showy. There are many other kinds as well and each has its individual charm, but the large-flowered white kind is the showiest of all and the one most often sold by dealers.

Trilliums belong with wild flowers or ferns or grouped informally in drifts where they can be enjoyed as a surprise planting in shade. These

The showy trillium (*T. grandiflorum*) belongs in a natural setting.

are sometimes used for spring color among myrtle and pachysandra, but these dense growers soon choke them out. In front of shrubs or well placed near a rock intermingled with maidenhair fern they look well. They are not suited for cover where permanent foliage is needed, since the leaves deteriorate in late summer.

Moist soil with plenty of leafmold or humus and a well-drained situation in shade suit trilliums. The corm-like roots are offered by dealers in the fall, and these need 4 inches of soil for covering. Spaced 8 to 10 inches apart and planted in drifts rather than formal groups, they make a charming colony. It sometimes takes them a year or two to become well established.

Turfing Daisy—4"—Zone 4   *Matricaria tchihatchewi*

Turfing daisy is another of the plants used as a lawn substitute in hot, dry areas where grass is a problem. The finely cut foliage has a mossy effect when grown in solid masses. Plants grow 2 inches high, topped with tiny white daisies on wiry stems appearing throughout the spring and early summer. Like camomile, it can be walked upon and makes a good crevice or paving plant.

Turfing daisy thrives in poor soil in hot, dry locations, but needs the usual attention of soil preparation and frequent watering until established.

Twinflower—4"—Zone 2   *Linnaea borealis americana*

The man for whom this plant was named described it thus: "A plant in Lappland, of short growth, insignificant, overlooked, flowering only a very short time; the plant is called after Linnaeus, who resembles it." He was the great plantsman and botanist Carl Linnaeus. Actually, it is a modest plant making a tiny evergreen vining mat with twin pink bell-shaped flowers on 4-inch stems. The tiny bells are fragrant and when grown with other acid-loving natives it is a rare jewel.

It needs a moist peaty soil, a natural setting and shade. The margin of a planting of native material where it can be enjoyed at close range is just the place for it.

Verbena—8–12"—Zone 2   *Verbena bipinnatifida*

For hot, dry places there are several perennial verbenas that make low, trailing mats. *V. bipinnatifida,* from the Dakotas, has crinkly foliage on creeping stems a few inches tall and purple flowers which appear from late spring till frost. A faster-growing kind is *V. canadensis,* with reddish-purple flowers on 8-inch stems which make roots as they trail. It is free-flowering and vigorous and, like all the verbenas, will grow in sandy soils.

Well-drained locations assure their permanence. Full sun and ordinary soil are their only requirements. Increase by cuttings or division of the roots, or they can be grown from seed.

Violets—3–18″—Zone 2   *Viola species*

Where to begin in discussing violets is difficult to decide. Even the most casual remarks about these joyous flowers of spring bring forth the comment, "But what about the lovely blue-and-white one that I have been growing these many years?" To begin again, violets are vigorous and persistent and, however charming and appealing we consider them, they can become the weediest of weeds in the small garden if not restrained. But grow them we will, so they need to be used to best advantage—as ground cover in shady places. Almost every gardener has a few violets, but some are more desirable than others. Kinds are legion and they are found all over the country under varying conditions of soil and light.

Violets produce two kinds of flowers—those we see blooming on the plants and those we don't see usually—the greenish cleistogamus flowers

Rosina, a pink everblooming violet, is a favorite with gardeners.

concealed under the foliage, near the base of the plants. These concealed flowers, which are only rudimentary in their structure, do not open and are self-pollinated. When ripe, the pods pop open, scattering seed in all directions to a distance of several yards or more. This is the reason that violets are so weedy.

These beloved wildings are divided into two distinct types. The common violets we grow are of the stemless type, since all leaves and flowers rise as a rosette from a rootstock or runner. In the stemmed group, usually taller in habit, flowers appear in the axils or joints of the leaves, which emerge from an ascending or upright stem. Blooms vary in size, ranging in color from white to yellow through lavender and purple, some with distinctive markings and veining, and make these spring flowers most appealing. The fragrant cultivated violets of gardens are mostly of European origin.

Leaf pattern, in considerable variety, is a characteristic of violets. They may be heart-shaped, lance-leaved, fern-like, arrow-leaved, palmatic or primrose-leaved, and these are not all. Some of the common names indicate their natural homes (such as Eastern violet, field pansy, marsh blue violet) or tell us something of the bloom (as downy yellow violet, larkspur violet, or sweet white violet). They vary in height from a few inches to a foot or more. There are so many kinds native to all sections of the United States that it is pointless to list them. Those described below include but two native kinds and several favorite varieties of *V. odorata,* the fragrant, cultivated kind listed in nursery catalogs.

> **Bird's-foot** (*V. pedata*). Grow it in full sun, in sandy acid soil with quick drainage. The type has lovely lavender blooms and the bicolor form is a combination of dark purple and lavender. This is not a rapid spreader and combines happily with other sandy soil plants.
>
> **Confederate** (*V. priceana*). A much cherished kind for shade, it has large grayish flowers heavily veined with violet-blue markings and makes a good cover plant.
>
> **Double Russian.** A sweet-scented double variety, it makes a valuable cut flower. Foliage is nearly evergreen and it develops neat clumps for shady places.
>
> **Rosina.** Flowers are pink or old-rose, appearing in spring and fall. Restrained in habit, it can be used in moist acid soil in sun or shade as a dependable ground cover.
>
> **Royal Robe.** Rich violet-blue flowers of good size, it has a delicate fragrance.

Where space is available, plant carpets of violets in shade.

Sweet Violet (*V. odorata semperflorens*). A fragrant form, it flowers fairly constantly from spring on.

White Czar. A white companion for Royal Robe.

With few exceptions, violets are shade-loving plants and grow easily in well-drained garden soil. Some kinds, especially the cultivated varieties, need moist, rich loam to produce good bloom. Increase by division can be done in spring or fall or at any time during the growing season.

Wall Rock Cress—4–10″—Zone 3   *Arabis species*

These are essentially rock plants of trailing habit which adapt themselves readily as ground covers. There are kinds for sun and shade. Not particular as to soil and requiring little care, they have foliage of good texture and attractive flowers. For slopes, steep cuts in grade where grass is not practical, tops of walls and rocky situations, they make good fillers with aubrieta, moss pink, alyssum, and other kinds. A well-tended rock garden filled with choice alpines requires considerable care, but there are sturdy rock plants suited to wider landscape use, and arabis is one of them.

Cut back arabis after flowering for dense mats of growth.

A familiar plant to gardeners, *A. albida* makes mats of woolly-gray foliage about 4 inches tall with showy white blooms in early spring. The double-flowering form is particularly showy and delightfully fragrant. For sun or light shade, it needs only ordinary soil. *A. alpina* is smaller in habit and less of a spreader.

An evergreen kind (*A. procurrens*) forms rosettes of glossy leaves with showy clusters of white bloom resembling candytuft. Flowers appear in April and May on 10-inch stems. It spreads by creeping stems, thrives in sun or shade, and grows in almost any type of soil. A neat, attractive plant, it has many uses.

Plants are increased by root division in spring or fall. The mat-like types can be cut back after flowering to induce denser growth. This kind of maintenance requires little effort and time and keeps plants vigorous.

Whitecup—4″—Zone 6   *Nierembergia rivularis*

Often listed in catalogs but not too well known to most gardeners is this dwarf perennial called whitecup. It makes a creeping mat, not too dense, with creamy-white, cup-shaped flowers accentuated with yellow centers. For moist soil on slopes among even lower-growing kinds such as thyme or creeping mint, or making its way through Kenilworth ivy, this is a plant to grow and enjoy for just the right place. It is tender where winters are even a bit severe.

Moist soil and partial shade or fairly deep shade are needed for white-cup to thrive. Easily raised from seed, it can also be increased by division.

Whitlow Grass—3″—Zone 3   *Draba fladnizensis*

Whitlow grass is the common name used for these rock plants of the mustard family which are among the first to bloom in the spring. Commonest of them all is *D. fladnizensis*, a tufted plant 3 inches tall of mountain origin. The flat cushions of foliage form tight rosettes studded with clusters of white flowers in early spring. It is a useful crevice plant for full sun or light shade. Many species are listed by growers of rock plants, including *D. sibirica,* with pale yellow flowers, which serves as a miniature ground cover in sunny locations.

Alpines as a group need gritty, well-drained soil and a sunny location. Division of the rosettes is the way to increase stock.

Wild Ginger—6″—Zone 4   *Asarum species*

The lowly wild gingers of moist, shady woodlands, particularly the kind native to the West Coast and the European wild ginger, are often

Few ground covers can rival the texture of European wild ginger.

the answer for a ground cover in deep shade where the soil is rich in humus. Under trees and evergreen shrubs, in places where sunlight is shy, these creeping plants make an evergreen cover of rich texture and permanence, so well matted that weeds seldom appear. Our native eastern species (*A. canadense, A. virginicum,* and *A. shuttleworthi*) are unfortunately not evergreen. All the wild gingers combine effectively with wild flowers to make a mixed carpet planting in shady places, or in masses by themselves under shrubs and trees. These plants spread by creeping rootstocks. Leaves are roughly heart-shaped and leathery in texture. In both city and suburban gardens, these evergreen forms are of considerable value where their soil requirements can be met.

Moist, rich soil with ample humus and a shady location are needed, but ordinary garden soils can be improved with peat and compost to meet this requirement. Increase is by cuttings of the creeping rootstocks with roots attached, or clumps from dealers.

Wintercreeper—2–12″—Zone 4   *Euonymus*

Euonymus is a familiar name to gardeners, for this tribe contributes greatly to the beauty of home grounds throughout the country. Not the least important are the evergreen forms, known as wintercreepers, which make excellent ground covers. They are extremely hardy, are vigorous in growth, maintain a fresh appearance throughout the year, and grow well in both sun and shade.

Unfortunately, they are subject to scale insects, which require considerable spraying to eradicate once infestation occurs. If neglected, these scaly pests spread rapidly, causing the plants to become unsightly as they lose their foliage and may eventually die. To those gardeners who have grown euonymus and never have been troubled with the problem of scale, it may not seem like a serious matter. Yet, there is nothing more unsightly than a badly diseased planting. Apparently, euonymus scale is more inclined to affect plants on walks in hot, dry locations than when it is grown as a cover plant. However, when present, it spreads to other plants such as pachysandra, ivy, and bittersweet. Spraying at the proper time, with repeat applications, will control and eradicate this pest.

Ways in which the various types of wintercreeper can be used are many. Its deep-rooting habit makes it a good soil binder. For covering banks and slopes, for clothing rocky areas, under shrubs and trees, and as a lawn substitute in the shade, it is most valuable. It responds to shearing and clipping for tailored effects. Many of the evergreen forms of euonymus will climb on the trunks of trees and shrubs, as well as walls, if not restrained. Sometimes they can be used to camouflage tree stumps or rock piles.

The common wintercreeper (*E. fortunei*), sometimes referred to as *E. radicans,* is the toughest and most vigorous of evergreen vines. There are numerous varieties, because it tends to produce variations in foliage known as sports. By nature it clings to hard surfaces by means of aerial roots, often referred to as holdfasts. Some varieties are valued for their colorful fruits, others for variegated foliage or deeper color in autumn. Varieties of *E. fortunei* include the following:

acutus. Widely used form for ground cover, because of its small foliage; also a good climber.

argenteo-marginatus. A silver-leaved sport.

Euonymous *Emerald Cushion,* a patented variety, makes a handsome ground cover.

carrierei. Glossy foliage and showy fruits make this form useful for cover where height is needed. If allowed, it forms a sprawling shrub, but can be controlled by pruning to stay low enough for ground-cover use.

colorata. This form makes an excellent ground cover and turns purplish-red in autumn, changing to a deeper tone as winter approaches. A rapid grower, it makes a good soil binder on slopes since the stems form roots as they creep.

gracilis. White, yellow, and pink coloring in the foliage. The variety *Silver Queen* is similar.

minimus. Miniature-leaved wintercreepers include *Kew,* with ¼-inch
leaves, smallest of all and slow in habit. It makes delicate tracery
on rocks and walls and can be used to good advantage wherever
this refined evergreen foliage is needed. Use it in narrow spaces
between walks and walls, as a mat in front of a garden figure or
bird bath, or under some featured evergreen. Its use along the
sides of walks seems more practical than between steps, because
of the danger of high heels being caught in the rigid, clinging
stems. The baby wintercreeper (*E. fortunei minimus*) has slightly
larger leaves.

radicans. Widely used as a cover plant because of its rapid growth.

vegetus. Highly decorative with rounded, leathery leaves and showy
fruits resembling those of bittersweet, only smaller, this plant is
frequently referred to as evergreen bittersweet. It makes shrubby
growth 3 to 4 feet high, but can be kept lower by pruning. The
trailing stems root as they rest on the soil.

Running Strawberry-Bush (E. obovatus). A native trailing species,
usually less than 1 foot tall, it loses its leaves in winter but makes
a green mat quickly and provides an abundance of red foliage
and fruits during the fall.

Any well-drained soil is satisfactory for this sturdy evergreen which
thrives in sun or shade. However, it is apparently more susceptible to
scale in hot, dry exposures. Propagation is by division, pieces of the
rooted stems, or by cuttings which root easily in sand and peat.

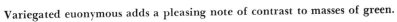

Variegated euonymous adds a pleasing note of contrast to masses of green.

Winter creeper makes rapid growth on a partly shaded slope.

Wintergreen and Salal—4–15″—Zones 2–5   *Gaultheria species*

Wintergreen, checkerberry, and teaberry are common names for a flavorsome evergreen ground cover found in woodlands over the greater part of eastern North America. Both the oval leaves and the bright red fruits which persist through the winter have a pleasant wintergreen flavor and are a source of this essential oil. The small, waxy, bell-shaped flowers, which appear in late spring, are partially concealed under the leathery, dark green leaves. Well suited to wild gardens or natural plantings as a carpet for acid-loving plants in shade or partial sunlight, it lends a charming effect wherever used. Under tall pines or spruces it makes a good mat, benefiting from the mulch provided by the needles of these trees.

Several species native to the West Coast have similar uses there as ground cover. Oregon wintergreen (*G. ovatifolia*) has leaves somewhat smaller than the common checkerberry. Western or alpine wintergreen (*G. humifusa*) makes a low, tufted mat only 4 inches tall. The popular evergreen foliage which florists call Oregon huckleberry is known in the Northwest as salal (*G. Shallon*). Used in poor soil on sunny slopes and banks, it makes an ideal soil binder, but grown in shade, it takes on the aspect of a sizable shrub.

Transplanting of sods in spring or early fall is the easiest way to handle the various forms of wintergreen. Lift as much soil as possible and prepare the soil well for its new home, using peat and acid compost. Water frequently until it is well established. Members of the heath family are synonymous with acid soil and require care in transplanting and plenty of water until well rooted. Since these are plantings for permanent effect, they merit special attention. Salal spreads by underground stems and is handled in clumps gathered in the wild or by planting rooted cuttings.

Wire Plant—2″—Zone 6   *Muehlenbeckia axillaris*

A miniature shrub from New Zealand that makes thick mats of growth formed by wiry stems with the tiniest of leaves, this is a good crevice or paving plant for sunny locations or light shade. It is sometimes used as a setting for the small-flowering bulbs. Not common, it is obtainable from rock-garden specialists. Zero temperatures without snow are likely to kill it. Another kind, sometimes called maidenhair-vine, or mattress-vine (*M. complexa*), has tiny heart-shaped leaves on dark, twining, wiry stems and thrives in poor soils, enduring salt spray. Although it has proved to be hardy as far north as New York City, until recently its commonest uses have been in the coastal regions of the lower South and on the West Coast.

Ordinary soil in full sun or light shade suits it. Increase is by division. One of its chief values is its ability to grow in poor, sandy soils, enduring drought and wind.

Woolly Yarrow—6″—Zone 2   *Achillea tomentosa*

Yarrows are generally thought of as weedy perennials for use in hot, dry places in gardens where space is abundant. The woolly yarrow is valued for its pleasing silvery-green, mat-like, evergreen habit and the showy heads of bright yellow bloom that appear in early summer on 6-inch stems. Where several kinds of ground covers are needed in rocky areas or sandy places, it is worth growing. It can be used among flagstones for it can be stepped on without harm. A form known as

Yellowroot combines well with rhododendrons and other evergreens.

Moonlight is greener in color, slower to spread, and carries flowers of a lighter yellow. There is also a compact form (*A. tomentosa nana*) of tight-growing habit with small white flowers.

Poor soil and a hot, dry location are best for this low perennial. Increase it by division at any time during the growing season.

Yellowroot—2′—Zone 4   *Xanthorhiza simplicissima*

A rather tall-growing, picturesque cover plant, yellowroot has had considerable attention from landscape architects but is little known to home gardeners. Native to the eastern United States, it is usually found in moist places. In habit of growth, it is most interesting, since the rigid stems carry their leaves in whorls at the tips. Purplish flowers of dainty form appear in nodding sprays before the leaves appear. Although not particularly showy in the open, the flowering stems lend themselves to rather striking line arrangements. As a ground cover, this is a plant well suited to moist soils, along streams and moist banks in sun or shade, or wherever the soil is on the heavy side. In autumn the foliage turns yellow and orange before it falls.

Moist soil makes the ideal condition for growing yellowroot, but it makes a good show under average garden conditions and is less invasive in dry soils. Propagation is by division or root cuttings.

Ground covers thrive under city conditions in the **Gardner Museum, Boston.**

5

Ferns Play a Part

Ferns are Nature's most widely dispersed ground covers. They appear in endless variety over much of the earth's surface and are found in all climates except the desert. In the wild they grow in both sun and shade and in various types of soil. Many spread by creeping rootstocks, making dense, mat-like growth, while others send up their fronds from crowns. The tall growers have dense, heavy root systems which cover sizable areas of soil and are deep enough to make useful soil binders.

Ferns as garden subjects are a source of continued interest and fascination from the time the fiddleheads unfurl in spring until they turn gold and brown in late autumn. In fact, once given the right location, ferns grow from year to year with so little attention that we take them for granted. They are of inestimable value for creating finished effects in a single season and make good dividers between formal and informal plantings.

Planted in groups or singly, they supply needed filler material under shrubs or trees. The tall growers can often take the place of low shrubs, since their height and habit of growth is certain, once they are established. When used with rhododendrons and azaleas and the various kinds of broad-leaved evergreens, they aid greatly in keeping the soil cool and moist, as well as adding materially to the finished appearance of the planting. As companions for wild flowers or to make a background for native plants, they have real merit. They also lend the shade needed by some of the smaller kinds, native to high altitudes, which tend to sulk in gardens in the heat of summer. Use them to break solid plantings of ground covers on banks and slopes. For northern exposures along the sides of buildings, they often prove successful when other plants fail for lack of light. The evergreen kinds have added value, since they make desirable permanent cover and are a most welcome sight in winter.

City gardeners have learned to use ferns in dark, shady places largely because they have seen them in old gardens where well-established colonies have proved their ability to persist for half a century or more, despite neglect. In the Victorian era, the study of ferns became a popular phase of Nature study. Ferns were grown indoors as house plants or in wardian cases. Rockeries of rather unnatural form were built in gardens under trees or near the walls of buildings where sunlight was scarce or absent. Into these man-made settings, clumps of native ferns were introduced. That they flourished and have persisted is evident by the large plantings still to be found. Nurserymen now list the commoner kinds in their catalogs and specialists in native plants feature them. In fact, for easy maintenance, more ferns can well be used on grounds because of their easy culture, their graceful and pleasing growth, and their tolerance of deep shade.

Ferns increase by creeping or running rootstocks, or enlarging their crowns, as with common types of perennials. The spores which appear in brownish sacks either on the reverse of the fronds or on separate stems are another means of perpetuation. Raising plants from spores has proved to be great fun for avid gardeners.

Ferns are usually transplanted in spring or fall. Actually, many kinds can be moved at almost any time during the growing season if they are handled with sufficient care to protect the fronds from damage. However, if this aspect is not important, fronds damaged in moving can be cut back. Some send forth new growth the same year. Many ferns have wide-spreading and fairly deep roots, which means that they must be dug with a sharp spade. In planting, set the crowns no deeper than they originally grew. Get them off to a good start by digging large holes to accommodate the roots without crowding. Woods soil, leafmold, or peat added to the mixture in which they are set pays dividends. Matting types can be lifted like sod and divided or replanted without breaking the roots. A good supply of humus added to the soil before planting is desirable. Water as you would any newly set plants until they are established. Plants can be obtained from dealers or collected in the wild.

Royal fern (*Osmunda regalis*) flourishes in shady corners of city gardens.

American Maidenhair Fern (*Adiantum pedatum*)—2'

Undoubtedly one of the most beautiful of our native ferns, it thrives in rich, moist, humusy soil. Give it a shady location, but not too dense. The flat fronds, arranged like a horse-shoe on slender, dark stalks, are lacy and delicate in texture. It spreads by creeping rootstocks and makes a superb ground cover. Planted at the base of a large rock or a wall, or combined with trilliums and other spring wild flowers, it makes a charming combination. This fern also makes a pleasing foreground planting for the bolder foliage of rhododendrons and other broad-leaved evergreens.

Berry Bladder-Fern (*Cystopteris bulbifera*)—2–3'

This unusual fern, with gracefully tapering, dainty fronds, forms bulblets on the under surfaces of the fronds which drop to start new plants. It also increases by its creeping rootstocks. Found in moist soil in shade, it produces long streamer-like fronds and is often seen hanging on the edges of limestone rocks. Although the berry bladder-fern can take situations somewhat on the dry side, it does not grow as luxuriantly as in moist soil.

Braun's Holly Fern (*Polystichum brauni*)—2–3'

This partially evergreen fern is similar to the Christmas fern, but the glossy fronds are wider, longer, and spiny. Its gracefully arching habit is very pleasing and it makes an excellent ground cover for shade in moist soil.

Christmas Fern (*Polystichum acrostichoides*)—1–2'

Easy to adapt to garden conditions, even in the city, this is one of the most satisfactory of our evergreen ferns. The leathery green fronds are glossy and the fiddleheads are silvery-gray. It makes an effective ground cover alone or with other native plants. Although it spreads by creeping rootstocks, it is slow to multiply. Found in ravines and thickets and sometimes in fairly sunny places, it does well in average garden soil but is much more vigorous when humusy loam with some lime is provided.

Cinnamon Fern (*Osmunda cinnamomea*)—3–4'

A denizen of boggy ground, it flourishes in moist soil and will take a fair amount of sun. The fertile fronds are golden cinnamon in spring, turning dark later. Somewhat coarse in comparison with other ferns, it

Maidenhair fern displays its fragile beauty against a stone wall.

Hay-scented ferns make a trim and pleasing effect.

is, nonetheless, decorative and useful for bold effects. Grown under tall shrubs or high-branched trees, it makes a good filler, often more desirable than shrubs of the same height.

Common Polypody Fern (*Polypodium vulgare*)—6″

A low evergreen of great beauty, it makes spreading mats on rocks and boulders, often in meager depths of soil, but fertile enough to support its luxurious growth. The leathery fronds curl up when dry, but respond readily to moisture and act similarly in extreme cold weather. Large mats are not always easy to transplant. It spreads by creeping rootstocks and small plants are best to start a colony. Polypody fern makes a delightful companion for the small wild flowers in shady places.

Crested Shield Fern (*Dryopteris cristata*)—2–2½′

A bluish-green wood fern, native to wet soil, it spreads by creeping rootstocks. Of pleasing vase-shaped form, the fronds are finely toothed and the effect is feathery. This is a stately fern for shade or half-shade in moist soil.

Ebony Spleenwort (*Asplenium platyneuron*)—6"–1'

A perky little fern, the slender evergreen fronds are noticeably narrow, only 2 inches wide. Because of its interesting habit of growth, it looks good in pockets of ledges. When combined with other plants, these should be small of habit so as to show to best advantage the beauty of the ebony spleenwort. Give it shade and gritty garden soil with leaf-mold. It can be grown in sun where there is fairly moist soil.

Evergreen Shield Fern (*Dryopteris spinulosa*)—2–3'

The evergreen, lacy-cut fronds are often used by florists. It is sometimes referred to as the spinulose shield-fern. There are several closely related kinds, and all are highly ornamental and of special importance in the small garden because of their evergreen foliage. Fronds rise from crowns. The evergreen wood fern grows in moist garden soil in partial shade, and is not averse to lime.

Goldie's Fern (*Dryopteris goldiana*)—2½–4'

Often called the giant of wood ferns, the large fronds are distinctly golden-green in appearance. Give it moist soil and a shady location in partial shade. Truly striking in appearance, this big-scale plant is for gardens with plenty of space. A single plant rising out of a low evergreen cover can be most effective.

Hartford or Climbing Fern (*Lygodium palmatum*)—4"

A fascinating fern, it hardly looks like one and grows as a vine. It needs moist, acid soil and can take fairly dense shade, but a little sunlight will not hurt it. Planted at the base of a rock where it is assured of needed moisture, it becomes a curiosity in the garden, but hardly a dense ground cover.

Hay-Scented Fern (*Dennstaedtia punctilobula*)—2'

Lacy and delicate, this widely known fern is easily recognized by its yellow-green fronds. Like the lady fern, it is native to upland pastures and makes a good ground cover. It can be gathered in the wild by lifting sods of the mat-like rhizomes. Cut these into sections and space 8 to 10 inches apart, covering them no deeper than they originally grew.

Interrupted Fern (*Osmunda claytoniana*)—3–4'

Extremely decorative where tall ferns can be used and most adaptable in city gardens, the interrupted fern is somewhat coarse but effective among tall shrubs. It is found along roads and the edges of woodlands in poor, stony soil on the dry side.

Lady Fern (*Athyrium Filix-femina*)—2–3′

This fern will grow almost anywhere it is planted. It makes a dense mass of growth when established and is sufficiently invasive to take over a given area if not controlled. Weeds have little chance with it. A fern of the open fields, it endures dry soil and sun. Of pleasing texture and graceful habit, it develops into broad clumps. If fronds become a bit worn in late summer, cut them back to encourage a new crop of light green foliage for autumn.

Maidenhair Spleenwort (*Asplenium Trichomanes*)—6″

Unusual and dainty, it is found in moist crevices of limestone rocks and needs lime to succeed. It forms rosettes of evergreen leaves on graceful wiry stems and spreads by creeping rootstocks.

Male Fern (*Dryopteris Filix-mas*)—2–3′

Similar to the marginal wood fern, but yellow-green in color, this and the lady fern are steeped in lore. It is native to rocky soil in woodlands, is semi-evergreen and leathery in texture. A shady location and garden soil meet its needs.

Marginal Shield Fern (*Dryopteris marginalis*)—2–3′

This evergreen woodland fern with fronds of leathery texture tolerates a wide variety of soils from acid to neutral. It can be grown in sun or shade provided that the soil is rich in humus. Blue-green coloring and a pleasing arching habit of growth make it ornamental and desirable wherever it can be used. It grows from individual crowns.

Mountain Holly Fern (*Polystichum Lonchitis*)—1–2′

Another species native to the Northwest, it closely resembles the Christmas fern and the Western sword fern. The fronds develop in clumps resembling a large evergreen bouquet. Ideal for a shady ground cover, it grows best in humusy soil.

Rusty Woodsia (*Woodsia ilvensis*)—4–6″

For sunny situations among rocks, this fern, with its fuzzy fronds in whorls, contributes the same gray-green coloring so characteristic of the native spreading junipers. Fairly easy to handle, but the root crowns must not be crowded when set out.

Sensitive Fern (*Onoclea sensibilis*)—1–2′

The segments of the fronds are rather wide and less deeply cut than many ferns. It can be cut back in midsummer to make a second crop of growth the same season. Since it increases by underground runners, it is a fairly rapid spreader. Good for banks or slope planting because of its dense rooting habit, it thrives in garden soil of average fertility and moisture.

Western Sword Fern, Giant Holly Fern (*Polystichum munitum*)—3–4′

This is the Christmas fern of the Northwest. It is taller with narrow evergreen fronds to 3 feet or more in height. A most useful ground cover for shade, the Western sword fern can be grown in average garden soil, but with abundant humus it is more luxuriant.

Viola *Jersey Gem* fits the crevices of the steps.

6

Adaptable Vines

Vines can be utilized as ground covers in large areas where they have ample room to develop. Their prime value is rapid cover of banks and slopes where steep grades make upkeep a problem. Climbing plants are sturdy, deep-rooted types adapted to wind and exposure, and require little care. In some instances, striking cascading effects can be achieved to enhance the appearance of outcropping rocks or ledges. A number of vines spread by underground roots or produce roots along their stems, making them valuable as soil binders. Those of rapid growth, suitable for camouflaging fences and retaining walls, may be allowed to spill over on the ground of adjoining areas for cover use. Evergreen kinds such as bearberry, myrtle, English ivy, and euonymus are among the most desirable of ground covers.

In addition to their decorative foliage, the showy flowers of such vines as the sweet autumn clematis, the various kinds of morning glories, the climbing hydrangea, and others add materially to their value. Fragrance is another asset of the various forms of jasmine, clematis, and nasturtiums. The trailing roses make the most spectacular display of all, and some varieties do double duty with showy hips in the fall.

But not all vines can be used widely as ground covers, particularly on the small home grounds. Those that climb by tendrils and trailing stems usually prove to be a nuisance, since they encroach on shrubs and trees, creating a tangled mass. This fact must be carefully considered before planting any of the more vigorous kinds listed below. Others, like Hall's honeysuckle, are so rampant that they frequently become a serious nuisance, unless carefully restrained.

The following list is representative of the hardy vines generally suited to ground-cover use where space and the appropriate setting are available. Selection for the home grounds needs to be based on those best suited and the care required to keep them in bounds. Annual kinds are listed because of their value for temporary effects.

Akebia—15–20′—Zone 4 *Akebia quinata*

Attractive because of its refined foliage, 5-leaf akebia is valued for its rampant growth for screening, and it makes a useful cover plant in the right place. Grow it on banks and slopes or let it scramble over rocks or place it where there is room for it to spread without becoming a nuisance. Because of its vigorous growth, it is not a suitable ground cover for limited areas in the small garden. The 5-parted leaves are semi-evergreen and of delicate texture. Curious purple flowers which appear in clusters in late spring, although not showy, add a note of interest.

Akebia is suited to sun or partial shade and can stand windy exposures. Reliably hardy, except in the coldest parts of the country, it grows best in good garden soil.

Algerian Ivy. See English Ivy, Chapter 4.

Bearberry. See Chapter 4.

Big-Leaf Periwinkle. See Periwinkle, Chapter 4.

Bittersweet—10–20′—Zone 2 *Celastrus scandens*

This native vine, much admired for its colorful fruit, can cause woe to any gardener who plants it without knowledge of its persistence, vigor, and deep-rooting habits. In the right place, it can serve as good cover for rocky areas, rough ground, or on banks or slopes where erosion is a problem. Its top growth can be kept in bounds by frequent heavy pruning. Otherwise, it forms a tangled growth and its rope-like stems twine around shrubs and trees, often killing them.

It grows in almost any kind of soil and is hardy in the coldest parts of the country. For fruit, plants of both sexes are needed. Seeds germinate readily and this weedy habit of bittersweet must be noted also.

Akebia does double duty as a vine and a ground cover.

The lacy beauty of climbing hydrangea is repeated in the seed pods.

Black-Eyed Susan Vine—6'—Zone 4   *Thunbergia alata*

This bright-flowered vine has possibilities for much greater use in gardens for temporary ground and bank cover. It is a perennial, native of South Africa, but is generally treated as an annual in cold climates. By nature a trailer, it makes a pleasing carpet in sunny places with cheery blooms in white, yellow and orange, accentuated with dark centers.

Black-eyed Susan vine grows best in rich garden soil but does well under average garden conditions. Individual stems trail 6 feet or more in a single season.

Carolina Jasmine—10–20'—Zone 6   *Gelsemium sempervirens*

The fragrant yellow blooms of Carolina jasmine, borne in clusters early in the season, and the neat evergreen foliage, are offset somewhat by its rather ragged appearance. But, used on banks or wherever cover is needed, the rangy habit is not readily noticeable, and hard pruning, after flowering, induces dense growth. It is hardy from Virginia south.

This vine is at home in sun or shade and is not partial as to soil, although it makes its best growth in good garden soil.

Climbing Hydrangea—30'—Zone 4   *Hydrangea peteolaris*

Where there is space and a rocky slope needs cover, or an outcropping of rock or a ledge requires softening, this vigorous summer-flowering vine may well be the answer. When planted near a stone or cement wall, climbing hydrangea eventually takes over and spreads widely on both sides of its support, making a most decorative ground cover. Although slow in getting established, it makes rapid growth, branching freely as it matures. The large glossy leaves are useful for creating bold effects and the panicles of white bloom in early summer are decidedly ornamental. Its ability to cling to hard surfaces by means of aerial rootlets is a point in its favor.

Climbing hydrangea needs only good garden soil and a sunny or partially shaded location. It is extremely hardy, drought-resistant, and relatively free of serious pests.

English Ivy. See Chapter 4.

Ground Morning Glory—3'—Zone 7   *Convolvulus mauritanicus*

A refined trailing perennial with stems 2 to 3 feet long, the ground morning glory makes a handsome mound of gray-green foliage. The blooms, of typical morning-glory form, are a rich blue with a white eye.

This appealing ground cover, valued for its free-blooming habit, is widely planted on banks, on slight inclines, and in parking strips on the West Coast. A tender plant, hardy to Washington, D. C., it can be used for temporary effects in cold climates when treated as an annual.

It endures heat and dry atmosphere with ease, and is adapted to a wide variety of soils. Stock can be increased easily from cuttings.

Hall's Honeysuckle. See Chapter 4.

Hartford Fern. See Chapter 5.

Ivy Geranium. See Chapter 4.

Jasmine. See Carolina Jasmine, Star Jasmine, and Winter Jasmine, herein.

Kudsu-Vine—3′—Zone 6 *Pueraria thunbergiana*

For difficult places where sun, wind, and generally poor growing conditions prevail, kudsu-vine makes a heavy foliage mass and rapid cover. It serves as a soil binder because of its habit of developing vigorous underground stems which travel rapidly. The purple flower spikes are not always seen because of the large, coarse, bean-like foliage. Well suited to warm climates, kudsu-vine is used in the South and Southwest. In the Northeast, it is hardy to New York City but dies back to the ground in winter.

Matrimony Vine—8–10′—Zone 4 *Lycium chinense*

A good soil binder, but a rampant grower, it suckers as it spreads and trails over the ground. The showy red fruits give it a decorative aspect, but it is one of those sprawling cover plants only desirable for rough places on banks or slopes where soil binders and quick effects are needed. Stems are thorny, which is an advantage for using it to discourage traffic. Hardy and of the easiest culture, it is not particular as to soil.

Moonseed—10′—Zone 5 *Menispermum canadense*

A vigorous native perennial, climbing by its twining stems, moonseed is a hardy, rapid grower, making a good ground cover where immediate effects are needed. Suited to poor soil, where little else will grow, it spreads by underground stems, making a useful soil binder, but because of its vigor it is also a pest when planted in the wrong places.

Morning-Glory—10'—Zone 2 *Ipomoea purpurea*

This popular annual vine makes good temporary cover for banks and slopes, and flowers best when grown in poor soil, in a sunny location. Flowers may be white, pink, blue, purple, or red, according to the variety planted. Because of its habit of reseeding, it can become a nuisance. It makes delightful cascading effects and dense growth.

Seeds have a hard coating and need to be soaked overnight before planting. When started from seed, plant where the vines are to be used, since this annual does not transplant easily. Plants can be purchased from local growers and are easily transplanted from pots.

Myrtle. See Periwinkle, Chapter 4.

Nasturtium—5–6'—Zone 4 *Tropaeolum majus*

A familiar annual vine for hot, dry places, it prefers poor, sandy soil for abundant bloom. Fragrant flowers in a variety of colors, soft-green foliage, plus a rapid-trailing habit make it a most useful ground cover for temporary effects. It tends to become something of a pest in warm climates, because of the ease with which it reseeds.

Best planted where it is to grow, it can be started from seed, or seedlings are sometimes planted in pots for transfer to the open ground. Despite its vigor and ease of culture, it is notably sensitive to cold weather and cannot be planted until all danger of frost has passed.

Periwinkle. See Chapter 4.

Porcelain Ampelopsis—10–15'—Zone 4 *Ampelopsis brevipedunculata*

Maple-like leaves and showy blue fruits in autumn give this hardy vine its appeal. A tough, sturdy plant, it is useful for rocky slopes, poor soil, and generally rough areas where it will not tangle with shrubs or trees. Planted in either sun or shade, it makes good growth and endures wind.

Rose. See Chapter 4.

Star Jasmine—10'—Zone 7 *Trachelospermum jasminoides*

Also known as Confederate jasmine, this glossy-leaved evergreen vine is cherished for its fragrant white flowers, borne in loose clusters in late spring and summer. Cultivated as a greenhouse plant in the North, it is hardy from North Carolina southward and is widely grown in the

Southwest and in California. It makes a most desirable ground cover for sun or shade. Pruning or pinching the twining stems induces dense growth to form a richly textured green carpet that serves admirably as a setting for the sweetly scented blooms.

Star jasmine can be grown in sun or shade in good garden soil.

Sweet Autumn Clematis—10–15'—Zone 5   *Clematis paniculata*

This fragrant flowering vine has great appeal because of its early fall flowers, silky seed pods, and glossy foliage. Unlike some kinds of clematis, it is extremely hardy, easy to grow, and generally most desirable. Give it ample space in a woodland setting, or on a rocky site or wherever its lacy effect is needed, in full sun or part shade.

Trumpet Honeysuckle—10'—Zone 5   *Lonicera sempervirens*

The showy trumpet-shaped flowers of orange, red, or yellow make this a most attractive vine. Foliage is coarse and mostly evergreen and it makes rapid growth. Where there is a place for it, this and other species of honeysuckle may be used to advantage in sunny locations or light shade. It is a sturdy grower, not particular as to soil, and endures wind and drought.

Virginia Creeper—30'—Zone 5   *Parthenocissus quinquefolia*

This familiar native vine and several related kinds are notable for their decorative foliage and rich autumn coloring. It makes a good ground cover for selected places, is extremely hardy, vigorous in its growth and not particular as to soil.

Weeping Forsythia—10'—Zone 5   *Forsythia suspensa*

This is hardly a vine, but neither is it an upright shrub. Rather, it is a most adaptable plant for cascading effects on banks and slopes where it can be placed to show its weeping habit to good advantage. Showy yellow flowers, clean foliage, and a graceful habit of growth are features familiar to gardeners everywhere. It is a special kind of cover plant for the tops of walls, banks, or large rocks.

Weeping Lantana. See Chapter 4.

Winter Jasmine—15'—Zone 5   *Jasminum nudiflorum*

Often more a trailing shrub than a vine, winter jasmine makes a good tall-growing ground cover for slopes and banks, since the arching stems root as they touch the soil. Clean foliage, dense fountain-like

Catmint (*Nepeta mussini*) with trailing roses on a bank.

masses of green twigs which are pleasing in winter, as well as cheery yellow flowers in early spring, make it a most desirable plant for informal use. Flower buds are often damaged or blasted in cold temperatures, but the plant persists with vigor.

Give it well-drained soil in full sun or light shade. Frequent pruning keeps it tidy.

Wintercreeper. See Chapter 4.

Rugosa roses bear their blooms from June until hard frost.

7

Useful Dwarf Shrubs

Dwarf shrubs, both evergreen and flowering kinds that do not exceed 3 feet in height under normal growing conditions, or that can be kept low by pruning, have a multitude of uses in present-day gardens. A goodly number fit the picture in landscaping contemporary houses, designed to hug the ground or blend with rolling terrain. Some are suited to extensive use on banks and slopes as soil binders. Those that are by habit slow-growing and broad-spreading, of even height, have the added advantage of serving as permanent ground cover. Because of their compact growth, they are easy to maintain and remain in scale with the settings for which they were planned.

Some of our most adaptable ground-cover plants fall into the category of dwarf shrubs, and because they are widely used in this way they are included in Chapter 4. Among them are the cotoneasters, heath and heather, pachistima, cowberry, the creeping junipers, and many others. Because of their woody stems, they are classified as dwarf shrubs. On the other hand, there are many others which can be adapted to ground-cover use or combined with carpeting plants for unusual effects.

Bayberry—3–4′—Zone 2   *Myrica pensylvanica*

The bayberry bushes found in rocky pastures and along the shore line from Newfoundland to North Carolina are seldom more than

3 or 4 feet tall, although plants are known to grow 8 feet high. A rugged shrub for poor soils, particularly those of sandy makeup, bayberry is useful as a sand binder for seaside gardens, or for dry hillsides. The clean fragrant foliage, picturesque twig habit, and gray berries provide interest throughout the year. Plants increase by stolons, rooting deeply as they make sizable clumps.

Give bayberry full sun and poor soil, and once established it will care for itself. Stock can be increased by division of the roots. Heavy pruning of old clumps will aid in renewing their vigor.

Bog Rosemary—1–2′—Zone 2 *Andromeda polifolia*

Bog rosemary, a low-growing native shrub of the heath family, is found in peaty bogs and along the edges of ponds, in the places where cranberries grow. The narrow evergreen leaves are whitish on the under surface, somewhat resembling those of the fragrant rosemary, hence the common name. However, the two plants are in no way related. It spreads by creeping rootstocks and makes a neater plant in cultivation than the specimens often found in the wild. The urn-shaped flowers which appear in May and June are pink, fading to white. A more compact form (*A. polifolia montana*), with smaller glossy foliage which turns bronze in the fall, blooms in early summer. Grow it with other acid-loving plants in moist locations or in a bog garden, where it can increase in its natural way.

Moist acid soil, rich in humus, is needed to grow bog rosemary. It can be used in full sun or light shade. Cutting sections of the rootstocks or layering are the simplest methods for home gardeners to use in increasing this shrub.

Box-Huckleberry—6–18″—Zone 5 *Gaylussacia brachycera*

Collectors of rare and unusual plants cherish the box-huckleberry for its evergreen foliage and its unique history. Most of the existing stock available today was propagated from a plant found in western Pennsylvania, believed to be one of the oldest plants on this continent. This member of the heath family is of notably slow growth, usually under 1 foot high, and spreads by underground rootstocks. It can be grown in full sun where its leaves have a reddish cast or in shade, provided that it is bedded in acid, leafmold soil.

Rooted cuttings or small plants from specialists need to be planted in well-prepared acid soil.

Bayberry is a rugged shrub for seaside planting.

Broom makes a beautiful display of bloom in hot, dry places.

Broom—6″–4′—Zones 5–6   *Cytisus species*

Several good stories have been told to account for the appearance of
Scotch broom in this country. However it arrived, it soon found a home
and has become one of the most decorative of soil binders. Because it
thrives in hot, dry locations in poor, sandy soils and develops sizable
roots, it is ideal for seaside plantings on slopes and banks or wherever
needed. Vigorous in its growth, disease-free and clean of habit, it endures wind and exposure to a remarkable degree. In areas where winters
are severe, not all types of broom are hardy—a point to remember in
selecting some of the hybrids, particularly, as well as those species native
to the warmer parts of Europe. Low-growing kinds of broom include:

Bean's broom (*C. beani*): Bright golden-yellow flowers on plants 1
  foot or more tall, of wide-spreading habit.
Ground broom (*C. procumbens*): Sometimes less than 1 foot tall
  or somewhat higher, with bright yellow flowers and dense matting habit.
Kew broom (*C. kewensis*): This hybrid form, with pale yellow flowers, grows only 6 inches high and makes a plant several feet wide.
Portuguese broom (*C. albus*): Under 1 foot high, with white flowers.
Prostrate broom (*C. decumbens*): Long, slender branches, of semi-
  prostrate habit, make a dense mat of growth covered with bright
  yellow flowers in May and June.
Purple broom (*C. purpureus*): Eighteen inches in height, with purple
  flowers.

Brooms need a hot, sunny location in poor, dry soil, sandy or gravelly.
Usually this type of situation is not too difficult a problem with many
gardeners who are searching for good ground covers. Plants may be
propagated easily by cutting in early summer or from seed. Container-
grown rooted cuttings make it easy to plant brooms, since larger plants
do not transplant satisfactorily.

Carmel Creeper—18″—Zone 7   *Ceanothus grisius horizontalis*

Carmel creeper, a low-growing form of the wild lilac of California,
has found favor as a ground cover on the West Coast. The dark, glossy
evergreen leaves and small clusters of blue flowers which appear in
spring make this bank cover desirable. It is also used under trees and
in broad masses for border planting. Plants average 1 foot or more in
height and can be expected to spread four or five times as wide. It
grows well in shade or full sun if kept moist.

Another species, the Point Reyes lilac (*C. gloriosus*) is more prostrate in habit with branches that trail the ground, rooting as it grows. Evergreen foliage, reddish stems, and pale blue flowers in clusters along the stems add to its appearance. It is most desirable for easy slopes and other places where flat cover is needed.

Average garden soil suits these creepers and they have no special requirements. Propagation is by cuttings.

Coralberry—3–5′—Zone 2   *Symphoricarpos orbiculatus*

Coralberry and Indian currant are familiar names of a widely planted, native shrub. The flowers are of little value, but the purplish-red fruits on gracefully arching stems are particularly showy in the fall. This plant suckers freely and makes a good soil binder, readily adaptable to slope planting. It is of clean habit, easy to grow and handle, but not particularly outstanding.

It flourishes in sun or shade and is not particular as to soil. Stock can be increased by dividing roots.

Drooping Leucothoe—3′—Zone 5   *Leucothoë catesbaei*

One of the most graceful and pleasing of the broad-leaved evergreen shrubs, leucothoe merits a place among ground covers because of its heavy root system, which spreads by underground stems. The arching habit of the branches, the lustrous quality of its foliage, which has few rivals among garden plants, and the showy flowers are other assets. This is a plant of year-round beauty, of particular value in winter because of the bronzy tones of the leaves. It can reach a height of 5 to 6 feet, but is not often seen that tall in the Northeast. Winter has a way of pruning it by killing back the growth, but it usually breaks from the base and is greatly benefited by pruning. Flower arrangers keep their plants in prime condition and keep it a fine ground cover by pruning it frequently for the graceful sprays of foliage.

Good garden soil, on the acid side, rich in humus, is needed to grow leucothoe. It grows in sun or shade, but is less apt to suffer winter damage in shady locations. It can be increased by dividing the roots or by cuttings.

Dwarf Japanese Quince—1–2′—Zone   *Chaenomeles japonica*

Dwarf forms of the flowering quince have the advantage of dense, twiggy growth, somewhat sprawling in habit, with glossy foliage and bright flowers. The spiny stems give it value for checking traffic where it is not wanted. These shrubs sucker as they develop and make suitable

Japanese holly serves as a tailored ground cover.

Dwarf yews add a contrast on this slope planting.

cover plants for slopes and level areas where this type of growth is needed. The *Alpine* flowering quince is usually less than 1 foot tall, with bright orange flowers in spring. *Knaphill* and *Rowellane* are hybrids of recent introduction. These grow to 2 feet tall, or even higher, with flowers in the bright red range. All the quinces thrive in ordinary garden soil.

Dwarf Willow—4″–2′—Zone 2   *Salix species*

Few gardeners know the dwarf willows, native to Arctic regions, which make excellent ground covers in the colder sections of the country. For poor soils, in sunny, windswept locations, these diminutive shrubs have considerable use, but they are, with a few exceptions, not easily obtainable. They are extremely hardy, and spread by underground stems. Some have silvery foliage and make a dense mat only a few inches high. Others grow 1 to 2 feet tall. The dwarf willows are fascinating to grow in places where they can be used to advantage.

Dwarf Yew—3′—Zone 4   *Taxus species*

Few evergreens have more diverse uses on home grounds than the various forms of yew. Dark green needle-like foliage, tolerance of shade, and a pleasing appearance at all seasons of the year give them an important place in any landscape scheme. They can be used in massed effects as entrance plantings for contemporary houses, on easy slopes, under high-branched flowering or shade trees, or wherever a high ground cover is needed. Properly spaced and well mulched, they develop into low, broad-spreading mounds, requiring little care from year to year.

A dwarf form of English yew (*T. baccata repandens*), often sold as the dwarf Japanese type, seldom exceeds 3 feet in height and spreads three or four times as wide. Among the Japanese kinds, *T. cuspidata densa* is slower growing and more compact than the *nana* form, making a plant about 2 feet high. The Canadian yew, particularly *T. canadensis stricta*, makes a most decorative effect in natural settings with its yellow-green foliage. This species is hardy to Zone 2.

Yews can be grown successfully in moist, well-drained garden soils in sun or shade. Compost or peat moss incorporated with the soil gives them the start that they need.

English Lavender—1–2′—Zone 5   *Lavandula officinalis*

Lavender is one of the best-loved of our fragrant herbs. A sub-shrub, usually listed as a perennial, it is grown in borders and rock gardens, and sometimes used as a low hedge. No herb garden is complete without it. The kind commonly grown (*L. officinalis*) and its various dwarf forms are not always hardy in the colder regions of the Northeast. The delightful fragrance of the gray evergreen foliage, which persists through the winter, the more potent scent of the flowers, and the whole aspect of the plant, plus its folk associations, make it a much cherished plant for gardens. A dozen clumps spaced 18 inches apart each way are the makings of a foliage mass as lovely as any spreading juniper in their silvery effect and a fragrant, sun-loving ground cover as well.

There are many horticultural forms of lavender, both natural hybrids and man-made, some with broader leaves than others, sending up flower spikes to 2 feet or more. Dwarf kinds easily obtainable are *Munstead,* with lavender flowers about 15 inches tall, and *Twickle Purple,* which grows about 10 inches high with rich purple flowers on a compact slow-growing plant. Other species for the collector to grow and revel in are numerous, but not easily available. Helen M. Fox tells about them with warm enthusiasm in her delightful book, "The Years in My Herb Garden."

Well-drained garden soil, even on the light, gritty side, in full sun, suits it best. It can be grown from cuttings or from seed, but most gardeners obtain plants bare-root from growers in early spring as field-grown clumps, or from containers. Go slow on fertilizer. Shearing the plants in early spring induces dense growth and division every three or four years keeps plants vigorous. Winter damage sometimes necessitates pruning to the ground. Lavender's lack of complete winter hardiness in cold New England was recorded nearly three centuries ago by John Josselyn, but, nonetheless, gardeners have been growing it and cherishing it all through the years.

Forsythia—3'—Zone 5   *Forsythia varieties*

Dwarf forms of several familiar flowering shrubs have considerable value as cover plants on banks and slopes. From the New York Botanical Garden has come a form of forsythia (*F. viridissima bronxensis*) that stays 1 foot high when fully grown. Of gracefully arching habit, with the familiar golden bells, small in size and durable, narrow foliage, it is of the easiest culture. A taller form, valued chiefly for its foliage since it is a shy bloomer, is *Forsythia Arnold Dwarf.* The stems of this mound-like plant root easily as they come in contact with the soil. Its maximum height is 3 feet and it can be counted on to be twice as broad. Because they require little or no care, both dwarf forms of forsythia can be used to good advantage on banks and slopes, for a soil binder, or wherever a shrubby plant is needed in broad masses or groups. Forsythia can be clipped or sheared for formal effects, is insect-free, and makes an attractive foliage mass until severe frost.

Ordinary soil, sun, or partial shade are all that it requires. Forsythia roots easily from cuttings.

Fragrant Sumac—3'—Zone 3   *Rhus aromatica*

This harmless cousin of poison ivy is a wide-spreading, low shrub with aromatic foliage sometimes used to cover banks or as an underplanting for shrubs and trees. It makes a good soil binder where a native plant is needed and keeps a most pleasing appearance throughout the year. In autumn, the foliage turns brilliant yellow and scarlet. Used on dry banks interplanted with native spreading junipers, it makes a harmonious combination. Hard pruning induces more dense growth. Where an evergreen winter effect is not important, it can be widely used for landscape effect, since it requires no maintenance. Tiny yellow flowers appear in spring, followed by red fruits.

Ordinary soil, even of poor, gravelly texture, suits it, and it grows well in sun or shade. Increase is by division of the roots.

Japanese Holly—1–2'—Zone 5   *Ilex crenata*

To cover a sizable area with any of the dwarf Japanese hollies would prove too costly. But, where low, mounded masses of evergreen foliage are needed in sun or light shade, this is a good plant to use. These hollies lend themselves to distinct pattern treatments with a mulch of pebbles, crushed stone, or pine needles as covering for the soil. Low-matting ground covers like thyme, moss sandwort, and creeping veronica may be used as carpets, but these require more maintenance. This type of landscape treatment, a modified use of plants as ground covers, is desirable where tailored effects are desired. The plants themselves can be allowed to grow in their natural form, but linked as a unit with the mulches suggested, are displayed to good advantage.

Slow-growing and compact, the smooth, leathery, box-like foliage of Japanese holly is one of the most rewarding features of this broadleaved evergreen. *Stokes* variety, *Green Cushion, Green Island,* and forms like *I. crenata nummularis, I. c. microphylla,* and the *Kingsville* holly are typical of the improved forms available. Because of their moderate rate of growth and mound-like habit, they rate high as desirable plants for landscaping.

Japanese holly needs fertile soil on the acid side with plenty of peat moss or leafmold incorporated. Because it is slow-growing, the balled and burlapped or container-grown specimens are not cheap, but are a good garden investment. They can be set out at any time during the growing season.

Mountain Andromeda—3–6′—Zone 4   *Pieris floribunda*

One of the truly notable broad-leaved evergreens, mountain androm-eda is widely planted wherever acid-soil plants can be grown. Mature plants range in height from 3 to 6 feet, but it is easily kept low by pruning. Because of its moderate rate of growth and its broad-spreading habit, it makes an ideal ground-cover shrub where height is needed. The showy spikes of white bloom are held upright and appear in early spring. Conspicuous flower buds add to its winter beauty. Particularly useful for combining with rhododendrons and azaleas and other broad-leaved evergreens, it makes a tasteful underplanting for dogwood, sour-wood, and other high-branched trees. For accent among carpeting plants, the laurel-like foliage makes a dramatic contrast.

Well-drained, acid soil with plenty of organic matter produces good growth. It can be grown in sun or shade. Stock is increased by cuttings and occasionally by layering of the lower stems.

Mugo Pine—3–4′—Zone 2   *Pinus Mugo*

Mountain pine is another common name for this alpine form of one of the most popular of garden evergreens. There are several varieties valued for their slow-growing, compact habit. When purchasing them in a nursery or garden center, select those with the smallest needles. A row of seedling mugo pines lined out in most any nursery will show considerable variation. Yet the selection of those plants that show the slowest rate of growth cannot assure you of acquiring dwarf forms. True dwarfness of habit is perpetuated when the plants are propagated by cuttings. These sun-loving evergreens are excellent for dry situa-tions among rocks or on slopes. Use them in drifts for billowy ground-cover effects and allow enough space for the full development of each plant.

Well-drained gritty soil suits these plants and a sunny location is best for the kind of rugged growth they make. They can be used in limestone soils.

Oregon Holly-Grape—1–3′—Zone 4   *Mahonia Aquifolium*

Like drooping leucothoe, this broad-leaved evergreen is kept low by severe winter weather. It is a spectacular plant in many ways, effec-tive for accent use because of its showy yellow flowers, blue fruits, and

Mugo pine fits this type of setting well.

Low-growing shrubs and carpet plants make a pleasant setting.

bold, glossy foliage. It increases by underground stolons and spreads fairly rapidly once established. Although it is a tough, sturdy plant, the foliage is often badly burned by the winter sun. Thus, it is best suited to shady locations in areas where frost penetrates the soil deeply. Plants reach 2 to 3 feet in height as they develop, but in the colder sections of the country they are often less than 2 feet tall. A lower-growing form (*M. repens*) is a good low-cover plant, less than 1 foot tall. It is similar in appearance, but the foliage lacks the luster of the taller form.

Well-drained soil in full sun or part shade suits this decorative shrub. Pruning to keep it vigorous and to eliminate winter burn serves to make growth dense. It is easily increased by division of the stolons, which root as they spread.

Rugosa Rose—4–6'—Zone 3   *Rosa rugosa*

Of all the seaside plants that endure salt spray and wind and poor soil, few can rival the rugosa rose. Its glossy, leathery foliage, showy blooms, and equally colorful fruits make it all the more valuable from a decorative standpoint. Spreading by underground stems, it makes an excellent soil binder. Although some varieties reach 6 feet in height, others average only 3 to 4 feet. Furthermore, it can be kept low by pruning, which also induces denser growth. Blooms may be single or double, from pure white to reddish-purple, and appear from June on. The large bright red fruits are ornamental throughout the growing year.

Rugosa roses may be combined with bayberry, sweet fern, dusty miller, and bearberry to create irregular drifts of richly textured foliage. For binding sandy soil on slopes or level ground, this combination of plants is both practical and highly ornamental. This shrub is equally decorative when used alone.

Hybrids of the rugosa rose are numerous. Among them are:

Agnes. Double pale yellow, fragrant. 6 feet.
Belle Poitevine. Semi-double deep pink. 4 feet.
George Will. Deep pink bloom in clusters. 3 feet.
F. J. Grootendorst. Clusters of bright red fringed flowers. 4 feet.
Frau Dagmar Hartopp. A recent introduction with silvery-pink blooms. Valued for its dwarf habit and attractive appearance. 18–24 inches.
Pink Grootendorst. Pink fringed flowers in clusters. 4 feet.
Sir Thomas Lipton. Semi-double, fragrant white flowers. 4 feet.
Stella Polaris. Single white blooms of good size. 4 feet.
Wasagaming. Double rose-pink, fragrant. 3 feet.

This rose requires no special soil, but planting with the usual care given any shrub gets it off to a good start. It blooms most freely in full sun but can be grown in partial shade. Increase is by division of the roots, which spread rapidly.

Sweet-Fern—3′—Zone 2 *Comptonia peregrina*

Shrubs with fragrant foliage are not numerous, but sweet-fern is one of them. The fern-like leaves are clean and attractive and this shrub spreads by underground roots, making it of value as a soil binder. Well-suited to dry locations and poor soils, it makes a pleasing companion for the low-spreading native junipers. Some nurserymen offer clumps collected from the wild, usually as fair-sized sods. It requires no special care once established, is of permanent value, makes a dense mass.

The following list includes a representative group of low-growing shrubs which have value for selective use as ground covers. Some are of special merit for their evergreen foliage, others for attractive fruits. Still others have spiny or thorny stems, often needed to check traffic along boundary lines of properties.

American Arborvitae (*Thuja occidentalis,* dwarf types)
Arrow Broom (*Genista sagittalis*)
Azaleas, low-growing kinds
Bayberry (*Myrica pensylvanica*)
Black Chokeberry (*Aronia melanocarpa*)
Bush Germander (*Teucrium fruticans*)
Chilean Pernettya (*Pernettya mucronata*)
Chinese Indigo (*Indigofera incarnata*)
Cutleaf Blackberry (*Rubus laciniatus*)
Dwarf Barberry (*Berberis buxifolia nana*)
Dwarf Boxwood (*Buxus sempervirens suffruticosa*)
Dwarf Bush Honeysuckle (*Diervilla Lonicera*)
Dwarf European Cranberry (*Viburnum Opulus nanum*)
Dwarf Myrtle (*Myrtus communis compacta*)
Dwarf Red Barberry (*Berberis thunbergi minor*)
Hills-of-Snow Hydrangea (*Hydrangea arborescens grandiflora*)
Japanese Boxwood (*Buxus microphylla japonica*)
Japanese Skimmia (*Skimmia japonica*)
Kirilow Indigo (*Indigofera kirilowi*)
Labrador Tea (*Ledum groenlandicum*)
New Jersey Tea (*Ceanothus americanus*)

Oriental Arborvitae (*Thuja orientalis,* dwarf types)
Rhododendrons, dwarf forms
Rose Acacia (*Robinia hispida*)
Running Swamp Dewberry (*Rubus hispidus*)
Scotch Rose (*Rosa spinosissima*)
Silky-Leaf Woodwaxen (*Genista pilosa*)
Virginia Rose (*Rosa virginiana*)
Warty Barberry (*Berberis verruculosa*)

Sweet alyssum makes an ideal temporary ground cover.

8

Annuals for Temporary Effects

Using annuals as temporary ground covers is often a quick and easy solution for erosion control, eliminating dust and mud, and toning up the rough appearance of a new property, devoid of planting. The cost involved is negligible and the effort expended is of little consequence in comparison with the results obtained and the pleasing effect on occupants and passersby.

New homeowners are nearly always confronted with greater costs for building than they had anticipated. Sometimes the moving of topsoil cannot be completed in time for permanent planting in a given season. Moving of trees and shrubs may delay plans for finished grading and seeding of grass areas. Additional construction such as the building of a pool or some feature in the garden may make it necessary for the family to live through an entire growing season without essential landscaping.

Occupants of summer places at the shore and in the country are often desirous of making their grounds attractive for a few months of the year. Permanent plantings may not be desired because of maintenance costs or initial expense of development. To meet these conditions, many low-growing and trailing annuals are ideally suited for effective carpeting and ground-cover use. They also provide an abundance of colorful bloom which, although terminated by the first hard frost, nonetheless serve their purpose as temporary ground covers.

Annuals like sweet alyssum, portulaca, verbenas, California poppies, and other easy kinds can transform a hot, dry slope in a matter of weeks. Some of the annuals listed below do well in shade. All are suitable for flat surfaces. Most important of all, practically all of these annuals do well in poor soil and many of them bloom more freely in soil of low fertility than when they are heavily fed.

Petunias are not described here in detail because they are so widely planted. For quick cover, no annual performs as well in its ability to spread, flower, and cover soil rapidly.

Several African daisies—such as the Cape marigold (*Dimorphotheca*), gazania, and arctotis—grow well in hot, dry situations and outdo themselves in bloom, especially when soils are sandy and poor in quality. These are best sown where they are to flower. Some florists offer them in small pots.

Quick-growing annuals for the shade to be used in broad masses for quick cover include forget-me-nots, monkey-flower (*Mimulus*), wishbone flower (*Torenia*), annual periwinkle (*Vinca rosea*), petunias, pansies, and godetia. For best results, it is practical to obtain small plants from local growers. This saves time in transplanting small seedlings.

Annual vines such as black-eyed Susan or clock vine, hearts-and-honey, Japanese hop, morning glory, nasturtium, scarlet runner beans, trailing lantana, and other quick-growing kinds can be used on slopes and steep banks for temporary cover. (See Chapter 6.)

Creeping-Zinnia. Listed in catalogs as *Sanvitalia procumbens,* it can be started from seed with ease. A trailing plant for sunny locations, slopes, banks or among rocks, the small flowers in shades of yellow look like miniature zinnias.

Dwarf Morning Glory. The variety *Royal Ensign* is an ideal low-spreading plant about 1 foot tall with deep blue flowers accentuated with a yellow throat. Full sun and ordinary soil suit it. Set plants 1 foot apart each way. It can be grown from seed or small plants can be purchased in flats.

Fig-Marigold. Listed in catalogs as *Mesembryanthemum crystallinum,* fig-marigold, also called ice plant, is a procumbent annual with pink or white flowers widely used on banks and slopes on the West Coast. It self-sows and makes a handsome display because of its dense matting habit. (See also Fig-Marigold, Chapter 4.)

Pinks. Varieties of the annual dianthus, usually under 1 foot in height, can be started from seed or obtained as small plants from growers. These do well in full sun in ordinary soil or among rocks.

Poppies. The California and Iceland types are among the showy annuals easily grown from seed in sunny locations for quick cover. Because the seed is as fine as dust and the young plants do not transplant easily, mix with sand and broadcast it over the area to be planted.

Portulaca. Also known as rose moss, this tough little annual is available in both single- and double-flowering forms. It is a brilliant and handsome carpeting plant only a few inches high. Seed mixed with sand and scattered in the area to be covered germinates readily. Once established, portulaca tends to self-sow and makes a desirable ground cover in hot, dry places, slopes and banks in full sun or light shade, between concrete strips in a driveway or along walks or in rocky areas. The plants bloom continuously until mowed down by frost.

Sweet Alyssum. Available in white, pink, lavender, and purple, it is one of the easiest of all carpeting annuals to grow. Seed can be scattered broadcast by mixing it with sand. Or, you can obtain small plants from flats and set them 8 inches apart each way to make an effective cover.

Verbena. This trailing annual with flowering stems, 8 to 10 inches tall, is available in separate colors or a mixture. It does best in light, sandy soils in full sun and requires little or no care after planting. Plants from flats or pots obtained from a local grower can be set out after frost danger has passed. These sturdy annuals often self-sow. Seed is slow to start, hence the reason for buying plants in flats. Space them 1 foot apart each way for good coverage.

Dwarf morning glory *Royal Ensign* is one of the most colorful annuals.

English ivy and periwinkle studded with autumn crocuses.

9

Soils, Planting, and Feeding

Well-prepared soil, the basic stuff of plant life, is the prime requisite for a good start with any plant set out on the home grounds. Ground covers are no exception. In fact, the places where they are often used are not always suitable for other types of plants. Most garden soils are either sandy or light in texture, clayey or heavy in substance, or a blend of the two. Some kinds are gritty or stony and there is no point in attempting to sift them to remove the stones. In fact, small stones are an asset for retaining moisture and checking erosion, particularly on sloping ground.

ORGANIC MATTER

Most garden soils lack organic matter, the essential component which retains moisture. Organic matter, or humus, is the fibrous material in soils that holds together the particles of sand, silt, and clay, and serves as the medium in which soil organisms function to break it down, releasing essential food to plant roots. It makes soil more easily workable or friable and the larger the amount of organic matter added, the greater the productivity that can be expected of most garden soils.

DRAINAGE

Drainage is vitally important to the successful growth of plants, even those that thrive in naturally moist soils. Flat surfaces where water tends

to stand after a heavy rain or during the winter can be drained by ex-
cavating the area and putting in a layer of gravel. If the area is lower
than its surroundings, raising the grade may be the answer. The problem of drainage often presents itself in heavy clay soils. Where it cannot
be corrected by improving the texture of the soil, agricultural tile
can be utilized to carry off surplus soil water.

If your soil is well-drained, of average fertility and good results have
been obtained with various kinds of plant material, it will require only
ordinary preparation and fertilizing before setting out ground covers.

IMPROVING SANDY SOILS

Where sandy soils prevail, the addition of organic matter in the form
of peat moss, rotted manure, leafmold, sawdust, or compost is essential.
These are also good mulching materials. See Chapter 11 for the easiest
way to handle them. Chopped sod is most useful for improving all types
of soil, but it must either be well decomposed or placed sufficiently
deep so as not to sprout. How much organic matter to apply depends on
the supply at hand and the area to be covered. If a sizable plot is being
prepared, any of the materials mentioned above can be scattered at
least 2 inches deep on the surface and dug in. When sawdust is used,
nitrogen must be added to compensate for what is lost as the sawdust
breaks down.

IMPROVING CLAY SOILS

Clay soils are composed of tiny particles that pack tightly and hold
moisture. They need organic matter to improve the structure of the
soil, to allow for the easier circulation of soil air, and to prevent the
soil from caking. Depending on the depth of the clay and the general
condition of the space to be planted, it may require 4 to 6 inches of
organic matter to condition the soil properly for planting. If time is
not a major problem, planting of a green cover crop for a season may
well be the solution. If the situation presents a major difficulty, the
best procedure is to obtain advice from your county agent or an ex-
perienced plantsman before attempting a large-scale project of landscaping with ground covers. When available, coal ashes are useful for
improving the texture of clay soils.

PREPARING SOIL ON BANKS AND SLOPES

On steep banks it is not advisable to turn the soil over as you would
on a flat surface or slight slope. Loosening large surfaces on slopes
hastens erosion or adds to an already existing erosion problem. In this

type of location, it is practical to prepare pockets of soil where plants are to be set as shown in the accompanying sketches. The depth of preparation should be sufficient to accommodate the roots without crowding and also to allow space for enough prepared soil to enable the roots of the ground cover to become established quickly.

IMPROVING POOR SOILS

In neglected shady areas under trees and along the sides of buildings where soil is known to be of poor quality (sometimes indicated by the appearance of moss), it is important to build it up as much as possible. Often competing roots of trees and shrubs that appear near the surface can be cut back hard without harm to the tree or shrub. However, there is no point in attempting to remove sizable roots such as those an inch or more in diameter.

TYPES OF SOIL

We usually speak of soil types as **acid, alkaline,** and **neutral.** Soils may vary, even in the small area of an average garden. For example, in a garden where the soil is known to be acid, the degree of acidity may be greater on a flat surface than on a slope where it tends to leach. Most home gardeners think of only two kinds of soil—acid or sour, and alkaline or sweet; soils which are neither decidedly acid nor alkaline are spoken of as neutral. The degree of acidity or alkalinity in soil is determined by a system known as pH. Soil reactions as revealed by simple chemical tests are expressed by numbers. For example, neutral soil has a reading of pH 7. Soil tests showing indications higher than 7 are on the alkaline or sweet side; those lower than 7 are on the acid or sour side. Soil tests may indicate an extreme condition on either side of the neutral scale, resulting in a toxic condition, but this is not a common situation.

Home gardeners are rapidly learning the advantage of soil testing, and there are kits available which are simple to use. However, the usual practice is to have tests made by competent analysts at the various county and state experiment stations.

A sizable number of plants adapted as ground covers prefer an acid soil or one with some degree of acidity. Others have a definite preference for lime, and a large group are not particular as to soil. Where soils are known to be acid, it is a good practice to choose ground covers suited to your own soil conditions. If some lime-loving kinds are desired, they can be planted in areas where lime can be added without injuring the acidity of the rest of the garden.

USES OF LIME

Lime is important to some kinds of plants because it corrects acidity in the soil, improves soil texture, aids in the liberation of plant foods, hastens the decomposition of organic matter, and provides calcium. (Lime is not itself a fertilizer.) Several kinds of lime are used in gardens. The two most common are ground limestone and hydrated lime. Ground limestone is slower acting but lasts longer than hydrated lime, which is usually best for quick reactions. When using lime, the gardener should remember not to dig it in at the same time commercial fertilizers or stable manure are added to the soil. This precaution is taken to prevent the rapid loss of the precious nitrogen through the liberation of ammonia when these substances are put together. In applying lime, simply scatter it over the surface of the soil and dig it in to a depth of 3 to 4 inches. The amount of lime to use depends primarily on the needs of your soil, which are not accurately determined by a soil test. Too much of it can be detrimental.

IMPROVING ACID SOIL

Many of our native plants, as well as azaleas, rhododendrons, and other broad-leaved evergreens and some deciduous plants, require an acid soil. While most garden soils need little preparation to make them suitable, it is sometimes necessary to increase soil acidity to grow acid-loving plants successfully. Acidity in the soil can be increased by the use of acid leafmold (easily made from oak leaves), hardwood sawdust, sulfur, and such fertilizers as ammonium phosphate, ammonium sulfate, and urea. Many home gardeners use aluminum sulfate, which is merely scattered on the ground and watered in. A soil test will readily determine the necessary amounts of these materials to use.

FERTILIZERS

Commercial fertilizers are the chief source of plant food for use on the home grounds. A "complete" fertilizer includes nitrogen, phosphorus, potash, and minor trace elements. The containers present formulas which indicate the proportions of the various elements used. For example, the formula 4-12-4 means that it contains 4 parts nitrogen, 12 parts phosphorus, and 4 parts potash.

Sometimes soil tests reveal a need for an abundance of nitrogen, or phosphorus, or potash. Nitrogen stimulates vegetative growth, and if too much is used an overabundance of lush foliage will be produced at the expense of blooms. Phosphorus is essential to root development and the production of roots, flowers, and fruits. Potassium has a balancing influence and is essential to natural plant development; its presence in the soil increases resistance to plant diseases. These three elements may be obtained separately in various concentrated forms, but they should not be used carelessly, lest they damage the plants.

Commercial fertilizers are usually dug in when the soil is being prepared. Additional applications may be made at any time during the year, but they are more immediately effective when water is applied afterward.

As a time-saver, fertilizing is best done while soil is being prepared. What to use and how much depends on your own gardening practice and the condition of the soil. Considering that ground covers are being planted for permanent effects, adequate fertilizing is essential. Organic types like rotted manure, dried manure, or any of the commercially prepared kinds such as dried blood, waste from sewage disposal, and others are frequently used, but these often need to be supplemented with balanced chemical fertilizers since they contain all the essential nutrients required by plants. Balanced commercial fertilizers with the formula for each kind clearly printed on the packages are easy to use. These should be applied at the rate specified on the container.

FOLIAR FEEDING

Concentrated plant foods which are readily soluble in water have made foliar feeding a popular method of feeding plants in recent years. These concentrates have merit for stimulating growth and there is actually little waste, since the liquid which falls on the ground is absorbed by the roots. Where an immediate effect is desired, foliar feeding, although somewhat costly, gives good results.

ACID-SOIL FERTILIZER

Acid-soil plants are best fed with what is commonly called evergreen fertilizer. This differs in its makeup from ordinary chemical kinds primarily in the type of nitrogen, which is an organic form. The use of this special formula has proved to be most satisfactory in home gardens, and it costs no more than other kinds.

PLANTS THAT REQUIRE A LEAN DIET

Fertilizing some kinds of ground covers actually does more harm than good. These plants, particularly the alpine types, which grow naturally in poor soil, should be grown that way in our own gardens. If given rich soil, they tend to react in a different manner, often getting scraggly, sometimes getting soft to the point where they do not survive open winters. Dry, sandy soils very often are ideal for the persistence, the perpetuation, and the free-flowering habit of these plants. To give a rich diet to a plant that has been used to spare living is often detrimental.

PLANTING TIMES FOR GROUND COVERS

The perennials, shrubs, and vines used as ground covers are usually planted in spring or fall. With shallow-rooted kinds or where any sizable planting is contemplated on an exposed, windy site, spring planting is often preferable, particularly in regions where winters are severe. Open winters in cold climates can do considerable damage to a new planting, causing the roots to heave. Fall planting is practical with almost any of the deep-rooted materials. Adequate mulching at either season is good insurance. (See Chapter 11.)

Actually, most ground covers can be set out at any time during the growing season if they are handled to keep the roots from drying out and given adequate water and care until the roots are established. Usually, spring is a busy season on the home grounds and setting out of large quantities of ground covers is a job that can be delayed until early summer or early fall.

SPACING PLANTS

How far apart to space plants is an important consideration. Spacing depends on the habits of the plant used and its rate of growth. It also depends on the size of the plants available and the immediate effect desired. Small, single-stemmed rooted cuttings require a longer time to become established than sizable clumps. For example, pachysandra can be spaced 1 foot apart each way, but it covers the surface much faster if spaced at 6-inch intervals each way. Periwinkle is more prostrate in habit, so allowing one plant per square foot is usually adequate. Ivy requires about the same spacing. Most of the alpines or rock plants used as ground covers can be spaced 1 foot apart each way. Crevice plants need much closer spacing.

Shrubs such as cotoneasters, junipers, and euonymus need at least 3 feet of space each way. The rock cotoneaster (*C. horizontalis*) can be spaced 5 feet apart because of its broad-spreading habit.

Most vines except annuals need even wider spacing, depending on the area to be covered. Trailing roses can be spaced at least 3 to 5 feet each way.

10

Care and Maintenance

Every growing plant has certain requirements as to soil, moisture, and light. If these are met, there is reasonable assurance that the plant chosen will grow and flourish without being coddled. Unfortunately, the tendency of some gardeners is to pamper plants. Then, too, they are impatient and expect them to take root and produce dense growth almost overnight. But this is not the way of Nature. Some plants require a fair amount of time to become established. Though sometimes they can be stimulated by fertilizer or additional water, this is not always the case.

On the other hand, there is the notion that ground covers are exceedingly tough, sturdy types of vegetation which can be simply planted and forgotten. This is not the case either, for there is the ever-present competition of weeds, besides the effects of sun and wind.

Weeding. The problem of weeding can be greatly reduced by the use of mulches until the ground covers have made a solid carpet. However, certain persistent weeds sometimes find their way among ground covers, and not the least of these is witch grass. If this pest, or any of similar deep-rooting habit, tends to overrun a planting, the practical thing to do is to dig it up and reset the ground cover. As long as the smallest portion of the roots remains, it will sprout and cause trouble all over again. Other shallow-rooted weeds can be removed by hand and this is

197

best done after a rain or while the soil is still moist. Much of this problem can be reduced to a minimum by early mulching with a mulch thick enough to keep the weeds under control. (See Chapter 11.)

Watering. Ground covers planted on flat areas are much more easily handled than those on slopes. Thus, thought must be given to giving adequate water with the right type of sprayer or a soil-soaker. Too much pressure results in unnecessary waste. On extremely steep slopes, it may be necessary to build ridges (as shown in the accompanying sketch) to keep water from flowing downhill too fast. Watering is only needed after planting and at intervals until the plants are well-rooted or during drought periods. When long dry spells occur in late fall, heavy watering is good insurance against winter damage.

Pruning. When first set out, plants obtained from nurseries are apt to be a bit rangy in appearance. Don't hesitate to prune them severely to encourage dense growth by causing new growth buds to break from the bases or crowns of the plants.

Plants like myrtle, bearberry, ivy, wintercreeper, and others may have long trailing stems. These can be cut back halfway to good advantage. Container-grown shrubs like cotoneasters, pachistima, and junipers, as well as most balled and burlapped specimens, are usually received in compact form. Vines in containers or bare-root vines usually benefit from some pruning at planting time.

The handiest tool a gardener can have when working among woody ground covers is one or more pairs of sharp pruning shears. Very often, plants need a little thinning here and there. This is best done with pruning shears rather than hedge shears. The purpose of pruning is not to shear evenly as much as it is to snip and to thin, to take out an awkward branch or a long, straggling one or keep a plant from becoming too invasive. This kind of thinning or pruning can be done at any time of the year. A rather ragged tangle of growth can be cut back to make quite a presentable effect in short order. Pruning done several times a year requires but little time. Often, pieces removed can be used for cuttings if more stock is desired or they can be used for decorative effects in flower arrangements.

Garden Housekeeping. Keeping ground covers clean in appearance by removing litter that blows in from roads and nearby trash cans is a minor item, but one that should be considered. Grass rakes, of either bamboo or metal, are practical tools to use in tidying up ground-cover plantings at all seasons of the year. Paper, heavy branches, and other kinds of débris are easily hauled out with the use of a bamboo or metal grass rake.

A well-mulched planting conserves moisture and controls weeds.

FOUR DIFFICULT PESTS

LACE BUGS

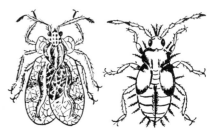

EUONYMOUS SCALE

Dormant oil spray in early Spring. Follow with malathion when insects crawl.

Yellow dots on leaves, use nicotine, malathion or lindane. Late May – early June

RED SPIDER

Causes leaves of perennials and shrubs to turn grey or yellowish brown Control with aramite or some other miticide.

FIRE BLIGHT

Stems appear dark with burned look. Cut and burn diseased parts. Sterilize pruners after cutting.

Sometimes, in summer windstorms or where tree growth is unusually dense, leaves fall and mat heavily. If not removed, they may breed disease. Needles of pine, spruce, or fir are seldom a problem, adding as they do to the buildup of a natural mulch. They also help to keep the soil acid.

Replacing of dead plants and increasing of stock to extend a planting of ground covers are part of general care and maintenance. Dividing of plants can be done in spring or fall, or any time during the growing season. Adequate watering is essential and, in some cases, temporary shading is necessary if the sun is unusually hot.

Pests and Diseases. Control of insects and diseases is usually not a major problem with most ground covers. Like all plants, during certain seasons they may be attacked by aphids or chewing insects. These are controllable with all-purpose sprays in most instances. Spraying or dusting should be done as soon as the damage is observed. The serious pests most likely to be encountered are fire-blight, various scale insects, red spider, lacebug, aphids, and chewing insects. The accompanying sketches indicate the type of damage caused by them, and methods of control.

Winter Injury. Damage caused by the effects of winter usually shows its effects in two ways. Shallow-rooted plants may be heaved by the effects of alternate thawing and freezing. This condition sometimes occurs in protected spots where the sun warms the soil quickly in spells of mild weather, followed quickly by sudden drops in temperature. The best kind of insurance in such areas is a light covering of marsh hay, or, easier still, evergreen boughs. Discarded Christmas trees and greens can be utilized to good advantage.

Winter-killing caused by the damaging effects of sun and wind on plants in frozen ground occurs more frequently during open winters. When the ground has a blanket of snow, little damage is usually apparent. The use of mulches (see Chapter 11), applied after the ground has frozen, aids greatly in reducing this type of damage, since the mulch keeps the ground temperature more even than if the soil were exposed to changing weather conditions. When carpeting plants and low-growing perennials are mulched, preferably with marsh hay, straw, or evergreen branches, they are protected from exposure to sun and wind. The techniques of winter protection are easy if good sense is used in the kind of materials used. The illustrations in this chapter suggest various methods for using winter cover effectively where it is needed.

Salt and other preparations used to cut ice on walks and driveways often do untold damage to ground covers of all types. These materials are applied to soften ice and snow and are usually shoveled to the most convenient spot. Frequently, they are dumped on a planting of periwinkle, pachysandra, ivy, or some small shrub. By the time the damage is discovered in spring, it is usually too late to do anything but dig out the area and replace the soil before putting in new plants. This point is made because the damage that results is often attributed to winter-kill when actually it was caused by salt.

Providing More Light. Some plants are by nature adaptable to a variety of soils and can be expected to thrive in sun or shade. In strong light they are usually compact of habit, whereas in subdued light they make a more lush, softer growth, sometimes thinner and more open in habit.

Very often, when ground covers are used in a shady garden, too much is expected of them. If shade is unusually dense, plants cannot be expected to grow and flourish as they would under average light conditions. These situations can be improved by thinning the overhead growth. Pruning of big-scale trees and shrubs often means the difference between success and failure, even with rugged ground covers. Overhead thinning to let in additional light does no harm to the tree or shrub involved if the pruning is done with care. Often, it is only necessary to remove a branch here and there to allow light to filter in.

In essence, easier gardening or landscaping with ground covers means choosing the right plant for the right place, giving it the needed attention when it is set out, and additional care until it is well-rooted. Once the average ground cover has taken possession of the given area, it can be depended on to hold its own. Most of the plants of low, matting, or trailing habit are by nature fairly disease-resistant, vigorous, and easy to maintain.

II

Making the Most of Mulches

Considering the term "ground cover" literally, the use of mulches belongs between these covers. To mulch means to supply a protective cover for the soil around newly set plants. It is a practice gardeners have adopted from Nature's way of forming quick growth on bare ground. Among the materials commonly used are peat moss, buckwheat hulls, sawdust, rotted manure, wood chips, oak leaves, pine needles, and others discussed herein. These materials are derived from some form of plant life itself—leaves, stems, flowers, fruits, pods, or roots. They keep the soil temperature even, conserve soil moisture, reduce the growth of weeds, and make it easier to pull those that appear. Mulches eliminate the necessity for cultivation and add to the appearance of a planting. Also, mulching newly planted ground covers and other kinds of plants is an easy and effective way to provide organic matter which most soils need. It is sound practice to use mulches in setting out large quantities of ground covers, since they reduce weeding considerably.

What to use for a mulch depends primarily on the type of area to be covered and what is available. When large areas need to be mulched, the item of cost must be kept in mind, as well as the amount of attention the mulch will need. For example, if sawdust is used, nitrogen must be added, since it pulls needed nitrogen out of the soil as it deteriorates.

However, once deterioration is complete, the nitrogen cycle is reversed.

To compensate for the loss of nitrogen in soils where such mulches as sawdust, wood chips, grass clippings, straw, hay, and corncobs are used, give the soil an application of complete fertilizer before the mulch is put on. Some gardeners mix nitrate of soda or ammonium sulfate with these materials before it is applied.

Feeding plants before mulch is applied, especially in large areas, is another point to consider. If the fertilizer is applied before the mulch is put on, time and labor are saved. The best time to mulch new plantings of ground covers is immediately after they are planted. However, if they are partially established and mulches are needed or desired to control weeds and conserve moisture, these are best put on in early spring when the plants are beginning their growth. How much to use is another important point to consider. If the mulch is not put on thick enough, it will not accomplish the purposes for which it was intended.

Peat moss is easy to handle and obtain. Cover should be at least 1 inch deep. The coarse, brown peat sold in bales is derived from sphagnum moss and makes a satisfactory cover. Peat from local bogs is often more desirable and sometimes can be obtained at moderate cost if purchased in quantity. The finer grades of peat are easier to break up than the sphagnum type and also easier to soak. Peat absorbs ten times its weight in water, and this point should be borne in mind when applying it. Never apply bone-dry peat to the soil as a mulch, or incorporate it with fairly dry soil, since the dry peat tends to pull the moisture from the soil as it comes in contact with it. It is essential to soak peat thorougly before applying it as a mulch or adding it to the soil.

Sawdust makes a practical mulch and is being more widely used by home gardeners throughout the country. Usually it is obtainable for hauling from any local sawmill. The coarse grade is preferable, because it does not pack together and crust as quickly. Fresh sawdust is apt to be unsightly when first applied because of its light coloring. However, it can be allowed to weather before using or it can be mixed with soil. Sawdust does not blow around easily and does not absorb moisture from the soil like dry peat. It allows the rain to penetrate and is gradually added to the soil as it deteriorates. If applied at least $1\frac{1}{2}$ to 2 inches deep, it controls weeds satisfactorily.

Wood chips make an excellent mulch for permanent use. Depending on the size of the chips, this mulch is slow to deteriorate and because of its large particles allows water to penetrate easily. It weathers in appearance as it ages and is rough-textured but not objectionable.

Well-rotted stable manure is ideal for level ground or easy slopes. It has the advantage of supplying plant food as well but is not always easily obtainable.

Leafmold in various stages of decomposition is a good and useful mulch. In its coarser forms, it can be used on slopes, especially if mixed with the surface layer of soil.

Pine needles, when obtainable, are the best of mulches for acid-soil plants, particularly the various types of broad-leaved and needle evergreens. This kind of cover is always good to look at and allows moisture to penetrate easily. If the mulch can be applied thickly enough, it can be used on fairly steep slopes.

Ground redwood bark is used on the West Coast.

Coconut fiber is another useful mulch where it is obtainable.

Oak leaves are a natural mulch for acid-soil plants. They break down slowly and have strong eye appeal as well for naturalistic settings.

Shredded sugar cane, often used for poultry litter, has its group of advocates. Although somewhat light in color, it weathers with age, and allows moisture to penetrate easily.

Straw, provided that it is free of seed, and salt marsh hay are adaptable and practical for large surfaces and sloping areas where erosion is a factor. However, these materials are fire hazards. As with sawdust, add fertilizer to the soil before the hay or straw is used.

Ground corncobs serve in areas where they are plentiful. Extra nitrogen must be added to the soil before the mulch is applied, and the general use of these has perhaps more disadvantages than good points.

Spent hops make a good soil cover but have an objectionable odor, although this will not be offensive if the material is not placed too close to windows or sitting-out areas.

Buckwheat hulls have long stood at the top of the list as an ideal type of mulch. The one objection to these is the expense of shipping, but the dark brown color and the light weight make them a joy to handle. As a mulch they absorb little or no moisture from the ground, allow the rain water and water from sprinklers and hoses to penetrate easily. They are ideal, because they are rich in organic content and they decompose slowly. Buckwheat hulls do not have any apparent effect on nitrogen depreciation in the soil. Gardeners who have used them for years simply add more each year, keeping the thickness of this mulch to 1½ inches with amazingly good results. Normally they do not blow except in exposed areas, but they are not practical on sloping ground, being too light in weight.

Grass clippings are desirable because they are easy to obtain and it is a good way to add the leaves of the most important of all ground covers to the soil. However, they are not particularly pleasing in appearance and they break down so rapidly that considerable quantities are needed to make a heavy application. During moist, humid weather they give off a rather unpleasant odor as they decay, and they pull needed nitrogen out of the soil, a point to be remembered. Yet, they add vitally important organic material to the soil. Two inches of grass clippings are also essential if the mulch is to have any real effect.

Black plastic film, aluminum foil, and tar paper have been used for mulches, and these, while quite effective, are hard to handle and not easy to look at. They are satisfactory and may be necessary on severe slopes where erosion is a serious problem. In limited areas strips of burlap may be used. All these materials are fairly costly if sizable amounts are needed.

Coffee grounds are rich in organic matter and contribute to the acidity of sour soils. People who use great quantities of coffee find it more convenient to put their grounds in a can in the garden until they have a sufficient amount, or place them where they can do the most good immediately.

For tailored gardens where flat areas need mulch, nothing is more appealing than **crushed stone, pebbles, or washed gravel.** These materials give a certain finish and pattern, as well as contrast to the surrounding planting. If certain color effects are desired, then colored gravel can be obtained. If light shades or white gravel or pebbles are used, the harsh effects can be softened by the planting of ivy or some other trailing plant which breaks the surface and makes a pleasing kind of tracery. This is a way of achieving unusual patterned effects.

12

Increasing Plants

Half the joy of gardening is derived from the pleasure of propagating plants to increase kinds that fit into the scheme of your own home grounds. With ground covers, the procedure is easy and the effort involved shows results in a comparatively short time.

Root division is the quickest way to increase many plants. The job

Dividing Perennials and Woody Ground Covers

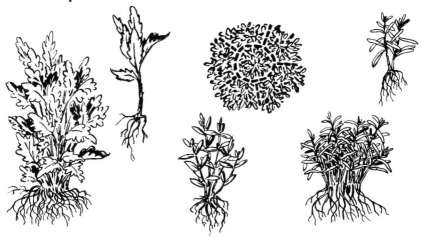

is usually done in spring or fall, but, as stated previously, most plants can be divided at any time during the growing season if given the needed care. Many ground covers root as the stems travel underground or along the surface of the soil. Thus, it is not necessary to remove an entire plant for division, since rooted pieces can be cut and moved to new locations at any convenient time.

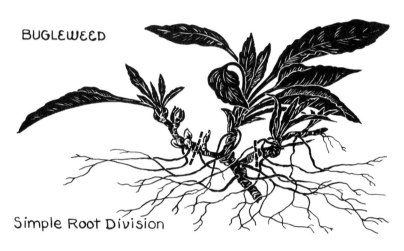

BUGLEWEED

Simple Root Division

Layering is an easy and sure way to propagate plants. The process means increasing plants by inducing branches to form roots while they are still attached to the mother plant. This is a natural method of in-

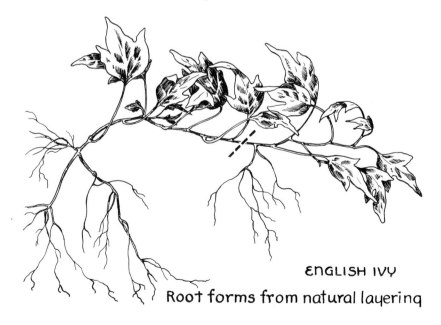

ENGLISH IVY

Root forms from natural layering

crease with many plants of prostrate habit. Results are most satisfactory when soil is in good workable condition and there is enough organic matter to aid in the development of a healthy root system on the branch that is in contact with the soil. Simple layering results in one additional plant, but if more plants are desired, the trailing stem can be pinned or covered at intervals or completely to induce roots to form along its entire length. Year-old growth is the most satisfactory for layering pur-

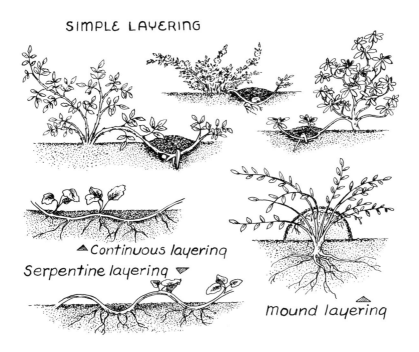

SIMPLE LAYERING

Continuous layering

Serpentine layering

mound layering

poses. This method may be carried out in several ways, such as serpentine layering, arching or tip layering, or mound layering. The ancient method of air layering for use on shrubs that are difficult to root from cuttings is another form. Details for techniques and handling all of these methods are shown in the accompanying sketches.

Starting plants from seed is one method of building a stock of many of the low-growing perennials, especially those generally associated with rocky settings. The procedure is relatively simple, but seedlings require care until they are fair-sized plants. It is a waste of time to start plants from seed unless the grower is willing to handle them with sufficient care to obtain a good supply of healthy seedlings. The steps as outlined in the accompanying sketches are offered for the benefit of beginners.

Method of sowing tiny seeds for even distribution

Drainage

— Soil mixture for seeds in pots or flats —
⅓ sifted garden loam
⅓ coarse sand
⅓ peat moss

After sowing barely cover with finely sifted soil and water with fine spray. Cover with damp newspaper until seed germinates

Sowing Small Seeds

Most seeds can be sown in rows. Depth to cover— 2-3 times the diameter of the seed

Label each kind. Tamp to firm soil and water gently but thoroughly. Do not allow soil to dry out.

Transplant when seedlings have 4-6 leaves. Firm soil with thumb and forefinger around each plant. Water and keep away from direct light until seedlings are established and then place in full sun.

Sowing Large Seeds

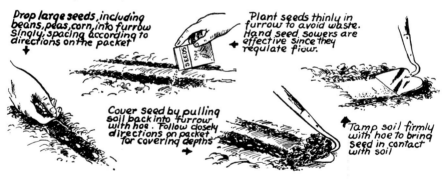

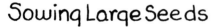

Drop large seeds, including beans, peas, corn, into furrow singly, spacing according to directions on the packet ↓

Plant seeds thinly in furrow to avoid waste. Hand seed sowers are effective since they regulate flow. →

Cover seed by pulling soil back into furrow with hoe. Follow closely directions on packet for covering depths →

↑ Tamp soil firmly with hoe to bring seed in contact with soil

Many woody plants are propagated by **cuttings.** Some kinds root easily by simply inserting them in soil, sand, or peat moss or in a mixture of sand and peat. Pachysandra and ivy are typical examples. Others require bottom heat and the use of root hormones to root successfully. Plastic propagating cases or electrically operated frames make the task of rooting the more difficult kinds fairly fool-proof. The step-by-step procedure of handling cuttings shown here tells the rest of the story.

Increase
by
Cuttings

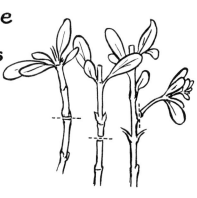

1 - Typical cutting
2 - Stem snaps easily

3 - Wrong type cut
4 - Right type cut
5 - Trim side growth

In Open Ground

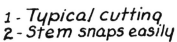

Remove lower leaves and re-cut base of the stem

Dig a propagating bed - remove soil - replace with sand

—6"

OR set cuttings in row in cold frame

OR Place plastic cover over frame. Moisture will collect on plastic and fall back

Appendix: Selected Lists for Easier Landscaping

Paving Plants

Miniature plants for use in the crevices of walks, flagstone paths, terraces and patios must be of compact habit and mat-like in their growth, and have the ability to endure traffic. It is an easy matter to pull up bits of sedum and tuck them here and there in the crevices, but these are seldom satisfactory. They are soft and succulent, and become slippery when trodden. Spaces between paving stones are sometimes a problem. Grass and weeds work their way into these tiny crevices, develop a well-established root system under the moist stones and become difficult to eradicate. If witch grass or any other deep-rooting kind gets a foothold, it is often necessary to lift the entire walk to remove these pests.

To attempt to grow ordinary lawn grass between these crevices is not satisfactory, because it can be kept low only where there is constant traffic. Where grass is used, corners and edges of walks need constant shearing by hand. Creeping plants that stay an inch or so in height are the answer. If there is considerable space between stones, use soil mixed with sand as a filler before planting. Those marked with an asterisk (*) can be walked on easily. The others in this list are suggested for decorative effects in corners and along the edges of paved surfaces.

Aubrieta	Kenilworth Ivy	Stone Cress
Auriculas (Primula)	*Mazus	Stonecrop
*Baby-Tears	Moneywort	Strawberry geranium
*Bluets	*Moss sandwort	Thrift
Bugleweed	*Mountain sandwort	*Thyme
*Camomile	*New Zealand Bur	*Turfing Daisy
Creeping Baby's-	Phlox	Wall Rock Cress
Breath	Pinks	*Whitlow Grass
*Creeping Mint	*Pussytoes	Wire Plant
Harebells	*Snow-in-Summer	*Woolly Yarrow
Houseleeks	*Speedwell	

Ground Covers for Seaside Plantings

Salt spray, wind, sandy soil often poor in quality, and exposure to rugged conditions are factors which restrict the types of plants that can be used successfully near the ocean. However, it is significant that most

213

of those listed below are distinctive in the texture of their foliage.

Bayberry
Beach Wormwood
Bearberry
Bergenia
Bird's-Foot Trefoil
Bittersweet
Blue Fescue
Broom
Cinquefoil
Cotoneaster
Creeping Baby's-
   Breath
Daylily
Dwarf Rosemary
Dwarf Willow
English Lavender
Evergreen Candytuft
Fig-Marigold

Fleece-Flower
Fragrant Sumac
Fringed Wormwood
Hall's Honeysuckle
Harebell
Heath
Heather
Houseleek
Juniper
Lantana
Lavender Cotton
Lily-Turf
Mat grass
Memorial Rose
Moss Sandwort
Mugo Pine
Oregon Holly-Grape
Potentilla

Roman Wormwood
Rugosa Rose
St. John's-wort
Sandwort
Savory
Silver Mound
   Artemisia
Snow-in-Summer
Stonecrop
Sun-Rose
Sweet-Fern
Sweet Woodruff
Thrift
Thyme
Verbena
Wire Plant
Woolly Speedwell
Woolly Yarrow

Ground Covers for Moist Soils

Moist soils or those that remain fairly wet over most of the growing season are suited to a limited number of plants. Woody plants and perennials growing under these conditions are usually found on hummocks which provide the essential drainage for their fibrous roots.

Baby-Tears
Bloodroot
Blue Phlox
Bluets
Bog Rosemary
Bugleweed
Bunchberry
Coral Bells
Cowberry
Creeping Mint
Creeping Snowberry
Daylily
Dichondra
Dwarf Willow

Fleece-Flower
Foam Flower
Forget-Me-Not
Galax
Goutweed
Hall's Honeysuckle
Heather
Labrador Tea
Lily-Turf
Low-bush Blueberry
Moneywort
Partridge-Berry
Plantain-lily
Primrose

Sand Myrtle
Sandwort
Speedwell
Sweet-Fern
Sweet Woodruff
Thrift
Trillium
Twinflower
Violets
Virginia Creeper
Wild Ginger
Yellowroot

Ground Covers Requiring Acid Soil

Many plants that thrive in acid soil are widely adaptable and often found where acidity is low or where tests indicate a neutral condition. The plants listed below include many members of the heath family which require acid soil in order to flourish.

American Barrenwort
Barrenwort
Bearberry
Bloodroot
Bluets
Bog Rosemary
Box-Huckleberry
Bunchberry
Cinquefoil
Cowberry

Creeping Snowberry
Drooping Leucothoe
Ferns
Galax
Heath
Heather
Japanese Holly
Mountain
   Andromeda
Pachistima

Partridge-Berry
Sand Myrtle
Trailing Arbutus
Trillium
Twinflower
Wild Ginger
Wintergreen

Ground Covers for Hot, Dry Situations and Sandy Soils

Plants listed here can withstand considerable dryness without damage. Once they are well established, they require little care except for pest control in a few instances. However, during extended drought periods, all plants respond to an occasional thorough watering.

Bayberry
Beach Wormwood
Bearberry
Bedstraw
Bird's-Foot Trefoil
Bittersweet
Black-Eyed Susan
   Vine
Blue Fescue
Broom
Cinquefoil
Coralberry
Cotoneaster
Creeping Baby's-
   Breath
Daylily
Dichondra

Dwarf Japanese
   Quince
Dwarf Rosemary
Dwarf Willow
English Lavender
Fig-Marigold
Fleece-Flower
Fragrant Sumac
Gazania
Gold-tuft
Goutweed
Ground Morning
   Glory
Hall's Honeysuckle
Heath
Heather
Houseleek

Ivy Geranium
Junipers
Kudsu-Vine
Lamb's-Ears
Lantana
Lavender Cotton
Lily-Turf
Mat Grass
Matrimony Vine
Moonseed
Moss Sandwort
Mugo Pine
Nasturtium
New Zealand Bur
Phlox
Pinks
Portulaca

Pussytoes
Rock Soapwort
Rugosa Rose
Sand Myrtle
Savory
Silver Mound
　Artemisia
Snow-in-Summer

St. John's-wort
Stone Cress
Stonecrop
Sun-Rose
Sweet-Fern
Thrift
Thyme
Turfing Daisy

Verbena
Virginia Creeper
Wall Rock Cress
Whitlow Grass
Wire Plant
Woolly Yarrow

Ground Covers for Shade

Shade-loving plants are of special importance for many home gardeners because of their adaptability to subdued light. A large number can be used also in sunny locations.

Akebia
American Barrenwort
Baby-Tears
Barrenwort
Bergenia
Bloodroot
Blueberry, Lowbush
Bluets
Bog Rosemary
Box-Huckleberry
Bugleweed
Bunchberry
Carolina Jasmine
Climbing Hydrangea
Coral Bells
Coralberry
Cotoneasters
Cowberry
Creeping Mint
Creeping Snowberry
Daylily
Dead Nettle
Dichondra
Drooping Leucothoe
Dwarf Anchusa
Dwarf Yew
English Ivy
Ferns

Fleece-Flower
Foam Flower
Forget-Me-Not
Forsythia
Fragrant Sumac
Fringed Bleeding-
　Heart
Galax
Gill-over-the-Ground
Goldthread
Goutweed
Ground Ivy
Hall's Honeysuckle
Irish Moss
Jacob's Ladder
Japanese Holly
Kenilworth Ivy
Leucothoe
Lily-of-the-Valley
Lily-Turf
Lungwort
Mat Grass
Mazus
Mock Strawberry
Moneywort
Mountain Andromeda
Oregon Holly-Grape
Pachistima

Pachysandra
Partridge-Berry
Periwinkle
Phlox
Plantain-Lily
Porcelain Ampelopsis
Primrose
St. John's-wort
Sand Myrtle
Sandwort
Sarcococca
Speedwell
Star Jasmine
Strawberry
Strawberry-geranium
Sweet Woodruff
Trailing Arbutus
Trillium
Twinflower
Violets
Virginia Creeper
Wild Ginger
Wintercreeper
Wintergreen
Winter Jasmine
Yellowroot

Ground Covers with Evergreen Foliage

Plants with foliage that remains green throughout the year are of prime value at all seasons, and particularly during the winter months. Not all the plants listed below are completely evergreen where winters are severe, but their foliage is of sufficient substance to be considered partially evergreen. Most of the perennials in this list fall into this group.

Akebia
Bearberry
Bog Rosemary
Box-Huckleberry
Braun's Holly Fern
Broom
Bunchberry
Carmel Creeper
Carolina Jasmine
Christmas Fern
Cinquefoil
Common Polypody
 Fern
Cotoneaster
Cowberry
Drooping Leucothoe

Dwarf Rosemary
Dwarf Yew
Ebony Spleenwort
Evergreen Candytuft
Evergreen Shield
 Fern
Germander
Hall's Honeysuckle
Heath
Heather
Japanese Holly
Lavender Cotton
Marginal Shield Fern
Mountain
 Andromeda

Mountain Holly
 Fern
Mugo Pine
Oregon Holly-Grape
Pachistima
Pachysandra
Partridge-Berry
Periwinkle
Sand Myrtle
Sarcococca
Star Jasmine
Trumpet Honey-
 suckle
Western Sword Fern
Wintercreeper
Wintergreen

PERENNIALS WITH EVERGREEN FOLIAGE

Barren Strawberry
Barrenwort
Coral Bells
Galax

Houseleek
Lily-Turf
Snow-in-Summer
Speedwell

Stonecrop
Woolly Yarrow

Ground Covers with Distinctive Foliage

Gray or silvery foliage, leaves with variegated markings and those with bronzy tones are of special value for contrast when tastefully used. Others with large leaves, the finely-cut kinds like the ferns and the extensive list with small leaf pattern are typical of foliage types among ground-cover plants. Fragrant-leaved kinds provide additional interest.

GRAY OR SILVERY FOLIAGE

Aubrieta
Beach Wormwood

Bloodroot
Blue Fescue

Dwarf Willow
English Lavender

Fig-Marigold
Fringed Wormwood
Gold-Dust
Ground Morning
  Glory
Lamb's-Ears

Lavender Cotton
New Zealand Bur
Pussytoes
Roman Wormwood
Silver Mound
  Artemisia

Snow-in-Summer
Sun-Rose
Wall Rock Cress
Woolly Speedwell
Woolly Thyme
Woolly Yarrow

VARIEGATED FOLIAGE

Big-leaf Periwinkle
Bugleweed
Dead Nettle
English Ivy
Goutweed

Heather
Lily-Turf
Lungwort
Plantain-Lily

Silveredge
  Pachysandra
Strawberry-geranium
Thyme
Wintercreeper

ACCENT PLANTS

Gray and Silvery Foliage, Variegated Foliage

Bergenia
Climbing Hydrangea
Cotoneaster

Drooping Leucothoe
Ferns
Juniper

Oregon Holly-Grape
Plantain-Lily

Aromatic Foliage

Bayberry
Camomile
Creeping Mint
Dwarf Rosemary
English Lavender

Fragrant Sumac
Fringed Wormwood
Gill-over-the-Ground
Lavender Cotton
Roman Wormwood

Savory
Sweet-Fern
Sweet Woodruff
Thyme
Woolly Yarrow

Native Plants Used as Ground Covers

Many of our favorite wild flowers are desirable ground covers, easily adapted to landscaping for naturalistic effects. The following list includes those discussed in Chapters 4, 5, and 7, as well as a representative number of native plants (marked with an asterisk, *). These have value for planting in wild gardens, but are not discussed.

*Anemone
 Bayberry
 Bearberry
 Bedstraw
*Bellwort
 Bittersweet
 Bloodroot
*Blue Bead Clintonia

*Bluebells
  (Mertensia)
 Blue Phlox
 Bluets
 Bog Rosemary
 Box-Huckleberry
 Bunchberry
*Butterfly-Weed

*Canada Mayflower
 Cinquefoil
 Creeping Mahonia
 Crested Iris
*Dogtooth Violet
 Drooping Leucothoe
*False Solomon's-
  Seal

Ferns
Fragrant Sumac
Galax
Harebell
*Hepatica
Jacob's Ladder
*Labrador Tea
*Mayapple
Mountain
   Andromeda
Mountain
   Cranberry

Oregon Holly-
   Grape
Partridge-Berry
*Pasque-Flower
*Pentstemon
*Pipsissewa
Pussytoes
*Rattlesnake Plantain
*Rose Anemone
*Sheep-Laurel
*Solomon's-Seal
Strawberry

Sweet-Fern
*Toadflax
Trailing Arbutus
Trillium
Twinflower
Verbena
Violets
*Wild Geranium
Wild Ginger

Flowering Bulbs to Combine with Ground Covers

Ground covers make ideal settings for the various kinds of small-flowering bulbs. Beginning with the snowdrop, the chionodoxa and the crocus and carrying on until the last autumn crocus has faded, these jewels of the garden provide color to enhance the beauty of carpeting plants. These in turn serve admirably as a background for bulbous flowers, especially those which appear without foliage. Then too, many of these miniature or diminutive flowers do not always have the proper setting in the average home garden and may become easily lost. Allowed to poke their heads through a carpet of foliage, they have a made-to-order setting which shows them off in all their fragile beauty.

The decaying leaves of many flowering bulbs, even the smaller ones, as well as the daffodils and species tulips, can be rather unsightly in the garden. However, when blended with the foliage of ground covers they are much less conspicuous.

SPRING-FLOWERING KINDS

Anemone
Camassia
Chionodoxa
Claytonia
Cooperia
Crocus

Eranthis
Erythronium
Galanthus
Iris
Leucojum
Muscari

Narcissus
Ornithogalum
Puschkinia
Scilla
Trillium
Tulip

AUTUMN-FLOWERING BULBS

Colchicum

Crocus

Sternbergia

SUMMER-FLOWERING BULBS

Bessera
Brodiaea
Caladium

Calochortus
Ixia
Lycoris

Tuberous Begonias
Zephyranthes

Ground Covers Suited to Florida Gardens

Only those ground covers marked below with an asterisk (*) have
been discussed in Chapters 4 to 7.

Agave
*Algerian Ivy
Artillery Plant
Asparagus Fern
Aystasia
*Bugleweed
Bur-nuts
Caltrops
Capeweed
*Carolina Jasmine
Coonties
Coromandel
Creeping Charley
Creeping Fig
Cuphea

*Daylily
*Dichondra
*English Ivy
*Ferns
*Fig-Marigold
Flame-Vine
Fog Fruit
Gopher-Apple
Hall's Honeysuckle
*Juniper
Lily-Turf
*Lippia
*Partridge-Berry
Peperomia
*Periwinkle

Sarawak-bean
Selanginella
Spironema
*Star Jasmine
*Strawberry-
geranium
Tick Trefoil
Trailing Fig
*Trailing Lantana
Wandering Jew
Wedelia
*Wintercreeper
*Yellow Jasmine
Yucca

Index